Management Communication

A GUIDE

Management Communication

A GUIDE

Deborah C. Andrews
University of Delaware

William D. Andrews

Houghton Mifflin Company
Boston New York

Editor-in-Chief: George T. Hoffman
Associate Sponsoring Editor: Joanne Dauksewicz
Editorial Associate: Jim Dimock
Associate Project Editor: Shelley Dickerson
Senior Manufacturing Coordinator: Marie Barnes
Senior Marketing Manager: Steven W. Mikels

PRINTED IN THE U.S.A.

Library of Congress Control Number: 2002109349

ISBN: 0-618-21415-1

123456789-QUF-07 06 05 04 03

Contents

How to Use This Guide

You can manage well only if you communicate well. That principle underlies this guide. In the chapters that follow, you'll find strategies for meeting such managerial and communication challenges as these:

- Too much to communicate: you know more than you can quickly and effectively convey to someone else.
- Too little to communicate: you don't know what to say.
- People who don't want to listen or to read what you have to communicate: they're busy, distracted, uninterested, convinced they already know what you're trying to tell them.
- Competing communicators and messages: others are sending stronger, clearer messages to the people you're trying to reach.
- Too little time: with all your duties, you can't find time to work effectively on your writing and speaking.

Benefits of This Guide

Managerial and communication challenges are complex. Like any aspect of managing, communicating in an organization can be muddled, highly charged, and confusing. In addition, as the practice of management becomes more intensely global, you're challenged to incorporate an international perspective in your communication, one that accommodates more than a merely decorative approach to cultural differences. As information technology expands, you're also challenged to take advantage of new media while avoiding the risks of such communication. Given these circumstances, you may have found that the one-size-fits-all dictates of many writing and speaking guidebooks fail you in all but the simplest contexts.

The advice in this book will support you in tough times—as you communicate and manage in a changing, complex, international environment. It is grounded in research and experience and centered on essential concepts and their implementation. It recognizes that communicating well is less about following guidelines than about knowing which guidelines might work in certain circumstances and when and how new guidelines need to be developed and applied.

As a manager, you make choices in your communication: about what to say or write, about whom to say or write it to, about what form to put the message in, about when to send it, about how to reshape the message as you receive questions and comments about it from the audience. Good instincts and experience help, of course, as you make those choices. But smart choices are not just a matter of instinct. By learning the management communication process discussed in this book, you can build a knowledge base; and as that base grows, you sharpen your instincts for communicating effectively.

What You'll Find in This Guide

After an introduction that establishes the model for management communication (you can read this in ten minutes), the guide is divided into two parts: Part I (Chapters 2–9) discusses the four elements of the management communication process; Part II (Chapters 10 and 11) reviews strategies for communicating in groups. Two appendixes address the conventions of business documents in expression and format, and a third appendix provides advice on two special communication situations of increasing importance to managers: handling the public and communicating in a crisis. The Website that accompanies this guide provides further examples, models, and suggestions for teaching and learning with this guide.

Organization of This Guide

Part I begins with an overview of the management communication process (Chapter 2), then describes each element in detail. The process begins with *analysis* (Chapters 3 and 4), in which you determine the outcome you desire, your audience's needs and expectations, and the best medium and timing for your communication. Based on your careful analysis of the situation, you *design* the communication product you aim for (Chapter 5). Then you *create* it (Chapters 6, 7, and 8). After that, you *verify* the product—you check to make sure it meets all your requirements (Chapter 9). Because they fall into a logical sequence, read these chapters straight through. But after you've done so, move back and forth to concentrate on a particular aspect you're finding troublesome as you draft a document or presentation. The Index will also help you find specific help fast while you compose.

The core chapters on creating communication products look at speaking and writing as a continuum in which you apply similar concepts of analysis and design. Chapter 6 describes the creation of visuals and texts, two products used both separately and together in presentations and documents. Chapter 7 foregrounds *spoken* products: interpersonal communication, meetings, and presentations. Chapter 8 foregrounds *written* products: memos, letters, e-mail, proposals, and reports. Chapter 9 discusses what happens after you've prepared the product as a draft and before you convey it to the audience. At this point, you pause and take a hard look to make sure what you've written or what you've outlined to present orally is what you want. You *verify* the product against your analysis and the design that follows from that analysis.

Part II, which, like the appendixes, can be read at any point, applies the principles of the management communication process to working in groups, whether on a large, formal team brought together to address a major project or in informal settings where you help colleagues shape their work. Chapter 10 offers advice on group dynamics and writing and speaking in teams; Chapter 11 discusses technological collaboration—how to use the tools of information technology to enhance teamwork.

Every chapter concludes with a scenario. These are not cases in the business-school definition but rather stories—narratives about communication challenges, based on real incidents but generalized to apply broadly. Recent research demonstrates that people learn most effectively through stories, and the scenarios tie together and apply concepts to help reinforce your learning. Suggested discussion questions highlight communication issues to consider or, better, to discuss in groups in or out of class. The scenarios also lend themselves to role-playing exercises.

Acknowledgments

We'd like to thank many colleagues for helping us shape this book, including our editor at Houghton Mifflin, Joanne Dauksewicz; JoAnne Yates, of the Sloan School at MIT (especially for her insights on genre systems); Melinda Knight, of the Simon School at the University of Rochester; Linda Driskill, Rice University; and Jone Rymer, Wayne State University.

The following reviewers for Houghton Mifflin generously provided comments on multiple drafts of the book: James Barker, U.S. Air Force Academy; Anne Grinols, University of Illinois; Betty S. Johnson, Stephen F. Austin State University; Michael Netzley, Singapore Management University; Diane P. Ramos, Duquesne University; Ronald Rice, Rutgers; Frank Sackton, Arizona State University; Anna Trosborg, The Aarhus School of Business (Denmark); Deborah Valentine, Emory University; Betty Vandenbosch, Case Western Reserve University; and Aline Wolff, NYU Stern School of Business.

Finally, we'd like to thank another group of colleagues—our students over many years. This group includes students at the Ohio State University, the University of Delaware, Philadelphia University, the College of Lifelong Learning at the University of New Hampshire, the Helsinki School of Economics, the University of Turku, and the International University of Japan. It also includes managers and technical professionals at several organizations, among them Battelle Memorial Institute, AT&T, GE Aerospace, Duffield Associates Consulting Geotechnical Engineers, Sun Refining and Marketing, American Chemical Society, Hercules Incorporated, the National Science Foundation, and the National Academy of Sciences.

Management Communication

A GUIDE

CHAPTER

Managing by Communicating

This chapter briefly explains two concepts that underlie the analysis and advice in this guide:

- You manage by communicating.
- Communicating is the purposeful exchange of messages among senders and receivers.

You Manage by Communicating

Managers talk with customers and employees, show graphs illustrating sales figures, send e-mails to colleagues across the room or across the globe, hold meetings, lead teams, sell products and services. In short, managers communicate. It's not something you do *while* you manage. It's *how* you manage.

Management Functions

Recall the four functions described in classic management theory:

- *Planning:* setting goals
- *Organizing:* structuring resources
- *Leading/motivating:* guiding people to act
- *Controlling:* checking to see if and how goals are met

Each of these functions is achieved through communication—and cannot be achieved without communication.

When an organization *plans,* it sets goals—for example, to make and market a product or service or to achieve some measurable outcome (profit, return on investment, market share). Planning requires negotiation and compromise among competing visions: Should we emphasize market share over profitability? Provide a service already wanted or create demand for one not yet recognized in the market? Subordinate short-term capital needs to long-term investments required to sustain financial viability? Answers to such questions are captured in words, pictures, and numbers by participating managers and then reviewed and debated to achieve a clear plan that expresses what a company wants to do. The plan may be reviewed by potential investors, used to attract key employees, and regularly publicized within the company to remind everyone of where it is headed and why. Planning occurs through communication as people speak and write, giving shape and focus to their vision.

The resources of the company—its capital, facilities, knowledge, public reputation, and especially people—must be *organized* toward the achievement of the goals the plan establishes. Discussions are required to align finances with goals—to put money behind intentions. People are assigned to tasks and grouped to reflect goals—for example, the sales and marketing staff, the accounting office, the production group. The organization of resources is typically shown in an organizational chart that enumerates the functions and indicates relationships. This visual representation communicates to all employees how their work is organized and where it fits into the overall picture. Written position descriptions further explain tasks and responsibilities. Words and pictures, in other words, drive the organizing function.

Leading or *motivating* workers to meet goals also occurs through communication. Senior executives express the vision of the company in presentations to investment bankers, politicians, and community leaders. Corporate logos (Michelin's tire-person, Citigroup's red umbrella) and mottos (General Electric's "We Bring Good Things to Life," FedEx's "The World on Time") give concrete representation to the central vision of the company. Managers routinely encourage, correct, and advise employees, using language (oral and written, verbal and nonverbal) to communicate and reinforce objectives and shape behavior.

In the *controlling* process, the company determines if it has achieved its goals by comparing results to intentions. Did we achieve the market share we sought? Have we reduced customer complaints as planned? Did we make a profit on the new product? Measurements of success or failure are often quantitative, but they are expressed verbally and frequently visually—communicated both as goals and as the results measured against the goals.

Communication Drives Organizations

The work of any organization begins and ends in words, numbers, and pictures. Sometimes the words and numbers are spoken and sometimes written. Often they are transmitted electronically—in e-mails and on Websites. The words may stand alone ("Great!") or may be combined into sentences or longer paragraphs or full reports. The words may come from one person or from a group. Numbers may be displayed visually with few or no words to explain them. Graphs or photographs may accompany verbal commentary or stand alone. However arrayed or transmitted, words and pictures do the work of an organization.

Communicating Is the Purposeful Exchange of Messages

Communication is so integral to everything we do that we rarely analyze how it happens. As long as it's working, we don't trouble ourselves with *how* it works. But if it doesn't work—or if we want to improve it—we can profitably analyze how we communicate.

A Simplified Communication Model

Communication is the purposeful exchange of messages among senders and receivers. Theorists have developed various visual representations of that exchange—communication "models" that allow us to separate and study the elements of communication. Figure 1.1 is a simplified version of many such popular models that captures the essential components and processes of any communication. While no linear display can fully represent the complexity and dynamism of even the simplest communication, this model highlights the underlying mechanisms.

Elements of the Model

Consider each element of the model:

- *Goal:* the purpose of the communication. Most organizational communication aims at one of three goals: to record, to inform, or to persuade. To *record* means simply to put the information on the record,

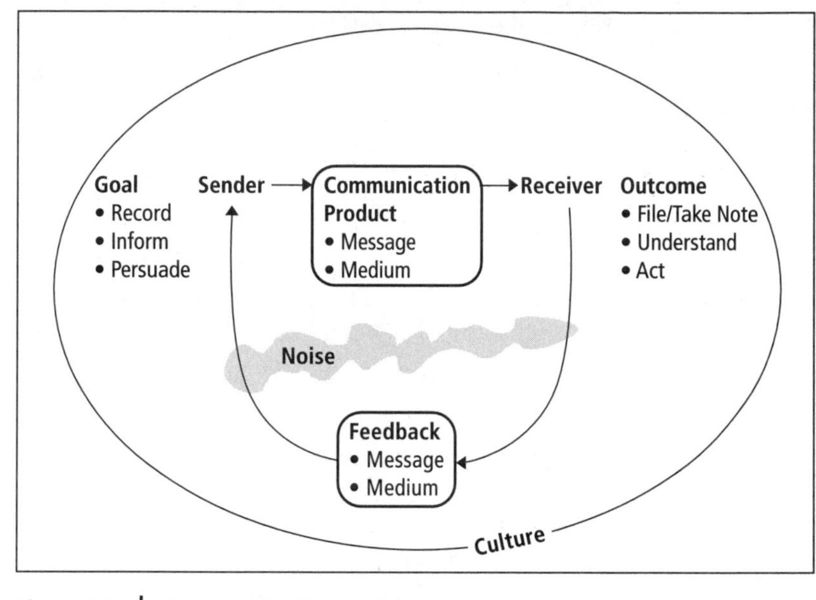

Figure 1.1 | Communication Model

to make sure it's available somewhere for someone. To *inform* means to let the receiver know, so he or she can do whatever is desired. To *persuade* means to convince the receiver to do what *you* want. Persuasion is the most typical goal of management communication.

- *Sender:* the person or persons initiating the communication to achieve the goal.
- *Receiver:* the person or persons receiving the communication.
- *Communication product:* the *message* (the information or idea being conveyed) and the *medium* (e.g., oral, written, visual) in which the message is embedded.
- *Outcome:* the result to be achieved by the communication. When the goal is to record, the outcome is merely to place the information on file, "on the record." When the goal is to inform, the outcome is to achieve the receiver's *understanding*. When the goal is to persuade, the outcome is to get the receiver to take *action*.
- *Feedback:* the message, embedded in a medium, that the receiver returns to the sender. The receiver of the original message becomes the sender of a message to signal, for example, understanding, ac-

ceptance, resistance, questioning, the need for clarification. Feedback promotes continuous negotiation between sender and receiver. (Note, however, that not all communications include feedback. A simple directive to someone to do something may achieve the goal without a return message from the receiver. See Chapter 4, pp. 38–39, for a discussion of the varieties of feedback related to different communication media.)

- *Noise:* the static that can impede the successful exchange of messages. Any distracting feature in the environment of the communication constitutes noise—from simple grammatical or spelling faults at one extreme to competing messages or dramatic events (e.g., a corporate merger or bankruptcy) at the other.
- *Culture:* the social setting in which the communication occurs. All communication occurs in a setting occupied by the persons sending and receiving messages. Culture includes both the immediate organizational setting (corporate culture) with its norms and traditions and the external society that affects conventions (language, for example) and standards of behavior.

Dynamism

Although some communications may be one-directional, most are circular. To reach a goal, the sender creates a communication product (embeds a message in a medium) for a receiver. But the receiver then becomes a sender by conveying back to the original sender another message, also in a medium. Feedback loops make communication circular. The cultural setting and the presence of all types of noise within the communication make the circular process dynamic. Multiple goals, multiple audiences, and multiple communication media also add dynamism.

Indeed, the two-dimensional space of this page prohibits showing the real dynamism of communication because the model appears linear: sender to receiver on one line, receiver back to sender on another. In practice, communication occurs in cultural settings and competes with noise as a large number of communication products in different media and often with multiple goals loop back and forth rapidly, almost simultaneously, each causing reshaping of the original product to the point where a truly new product arises. To visualize this, imagine not a linear pattern as shown in Figure 1.1 but a sphere formed by the many loops of the different communications.

Organizational Dimensions of Communication

The basic model is easily understood as it describes interpersonal communication: the exchange of messages between two individuals. Jose speaks to Juan, or Mary writes to Tom.

Managerial communication can become more complicated because it can occur among single and group senders and single and group receivers. There are four possibilities:

- *Single sender–single receiver:* an account executive speaks to a purchasing agent.
- *Single sender–group receiver:* an account executive speaks to a group of potential buyers.
- *Group sender–single receiver:* several persons make a proposal to a single individual.
- *Group sender–group receiver:* several persons make a proposal to a group of potential buyers.

The key processes of communication apply in each of these models, but they are carried out differently depending on whether the sender or receiver is a single person or a group. Management communication is frequently carried out between, among, and within groups—multiple senders and/or multiple receivers.

For example, a team of accountants may work together to produce a written report on suggested write-downs for nonperforming loans, and its group report might be sent to another group which will distill its results for a single executive. In the first group, communication occurs one-to-one among the members, but the final group report is conveyed to another group, and within it there are more one-to-one communications before a second group report is conveyed to a single audience. Situations like these, typical in business, require special attention to group dynamics and collaboration (see Chapter 10).

Communication Networks in Organizations

Within organizations, communications typically follow known routes, both formal and informal. Reporting relationships often define formal routes of communication: you write to your manager, who writes to her vice president, and so on up or down the chain of command. But much organizational communication follows informal routes. Good ideas often

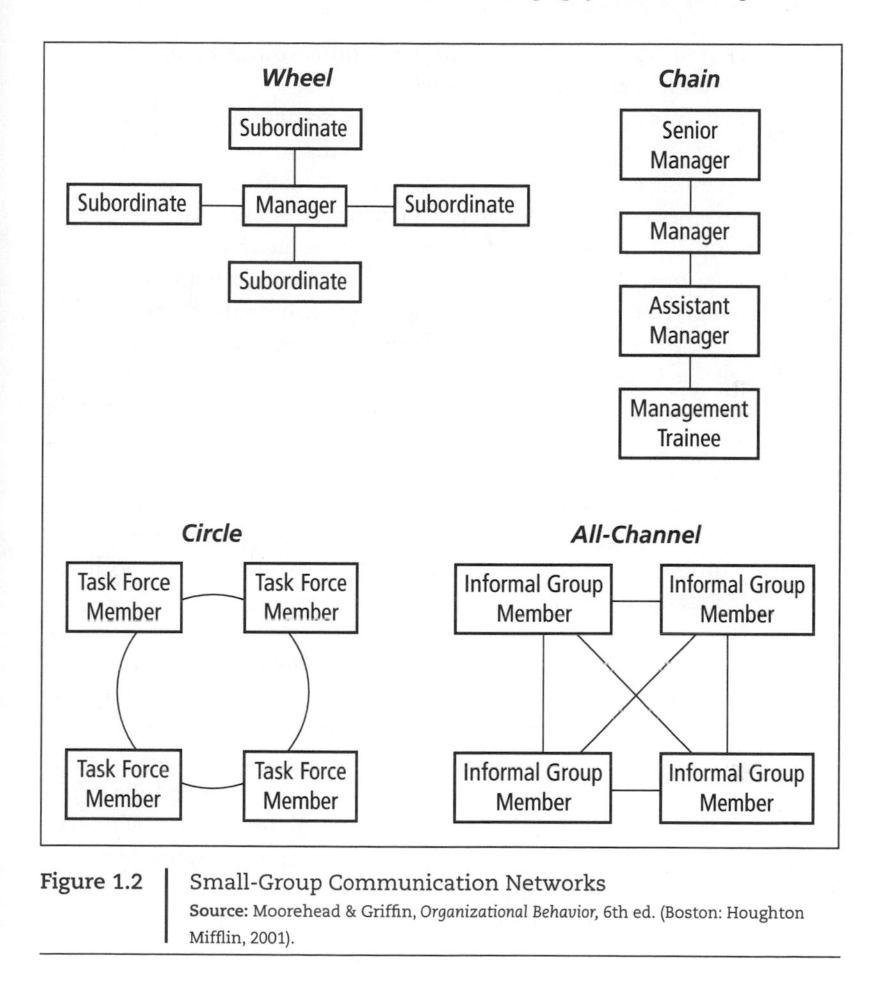

Figure 1.2 Small-Group Communication Networks
Source: Moorehead & Griffin, *Organizational Behavior,* 6th ed. (Boston: Houghton Mifflin, 2001).

emerge as people from different parts of a business gather around the water cooler or coffee station and exchange observations and proposals.

Whether the communication is formal or informal, networks emerge through which messages are sent and received. Researchers have identified four such networks (see Figure 1.2):

- *Wheel:* messages travel to and from one central person. The head of a division may send requests out to several persons and receive each individual's reply back to her, with no direct communication among the members of the division.

- *Chain:* messages travel from one person to another in a known sequence. A junior auditor might send his report to his manager, who forwards it with her comments to the lead auditor, who in turn forwards the report to the managing partner. Messages move in one direction, with no feedback to those lower on the chain.
- *Circle:* messages are exchanged among persons with similar responsibilities regardless of their organizational status. Within groups, persons working on the same problem might communicate freely back and forth, sending and receiving multiple messages as the work progresses but not communicating directly with others in the same group.
- *All-channel:* messages move back and forth among all members of a group as those members determine who needs to know what. Individuals and groups send and receive messages without regard to organizational or team status, reaching across lines of authority as information is developed or requested.

No single network is best or most effective, and every organization has a culture that privileges one or several types of networks over others. Hierarchical, bureaucratic organizations tend to favor wheels and chains, whereas open organizations are more apt to emphasize circles and all-channel networks. Special work teams formed to address specific problems generally communicate in circles and through all-channel networks as they proceed but might then follow a wheel or chain network to report their findings upward in the organization.

Identifying different routes or networks helps you understand how communications occur in specific settings and increases your awareness of choices that can enhance or impede communication.

SCENARIO

Deciding When and How to Communicate

Pekka Gallen manages a 14-person staff responsible for selling optical equipment to telecommunication companies worldwide. He is based in London, and his staff is deployed there and in Canada, France, Norway, and the eastern United States. Halfway through the second quarter, he calculates that his staff has booked only $8 million of the quarter's total sales target of $21 million. He feels pressure to meet the quarterly target, a task he can accomplish only with and through his staff and that requires a message telling them the current position, encouraging them to meet the goal, and seeking their advice about how to do that. The message has to balance facts with cheerleading, leading with collaborating.

Pekka reviews his options. Given the geographic dispersion of the staff, an e-mail message seems practical since it will reach all 14 persons at the same time across many time zones. An e-mail can also make the facts clear, and its tone can convey urgency. But Pekka wants to do more: inspire and motivate; encourage group brainstorming about how to increase sales; finally develop a shared strategy for achieving the quarterly target. A simple e-mail seems inadequate. Pekka feels he needs to be physically present with the staff, showing them through his body language and voice that they face a serious challenge but one they can jointly master. He needs to project leadership in a dynamic way not achievable through a collection of words on a computer screen. He also needs rich interaction and feedback—questions, answers, suggestions for action—that result from face-to-face communication.

The best plan seems to be gathering the entire staff in one room. But how long will it take to bring everyone in from the field? How much will it cost? What will be lost in sales calls the staff might have made instead of flying to a central location to spend time talking? Videoconferencing is an attractive option, but only two of his staff are at facilities with that capability; arranging for access for the others would take more time and energy than he wants to spend on logistics.

Pekka decides on a multilevel communication strategy. First, he sends an e-mail to his staff containing the sales information, issuing a crisp call to action, and requesting that each staff member post suggested strategies via e-mail to the group, not just to him.

After sending the e-mail, he meets face-to-face with two of the staff who work out of his London office and then calls each other staff member individually. After digesting the responses—those via e-mail and those from direct conversations—he summarizes the questions and suggestions and produces a plan of action based on them. He circulates the summary and the plan via e-mail and asks for further responses, both to him directly and among all the others.

All this takes a week, bringing the staff that much closer to the end of the quarter. Pekka decides after all that the cost of a meeting is justified and schedules a two-day "war conference" for a Saturday and Sunday in

London. He gives the staff a week's notice so they can arrange their schedules without interfering with their work—and to put pressure on them to produce additional sales to report at the meeting.

Questions for Discussion

1. How can the communication model help sort out Pekka's choices? Apply the model by identifying goal, sender, receiver, and media.
2. How do different communication media promote or impede Pekka's efforts to get results?
3. What are the advantages and disadvantages of using multiple communication media?
4. What communication networks does Pekka employ: wheel, chain, circle, all-channel? What are their relative advantages and disadvantages?
5. Does Pekka have one or several goals? Do they conflict or reinforce each other? How does his choice of media enhance or impede the achievement of multiple goals?

PART

I The Management Communication Process

CHAPTER

2 Overview of the Management Communication Process

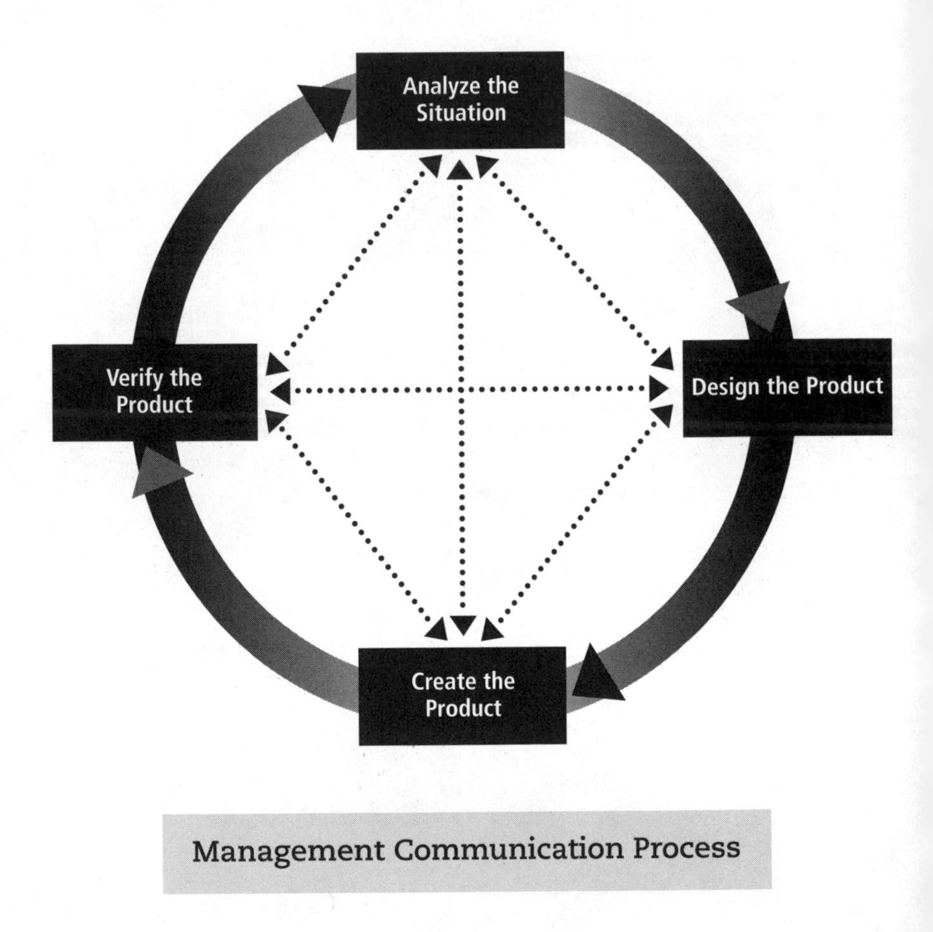

Management Communication Process

Like every aspect of management, communication is a process—a set of interconnected actions performed over time to achieve a goal. As with any process, when you're communicating—writing or speaking—you tend not to notice the process itself because you're focused on what you're trying to achieve. Your goal isn't a perfect process but an effective product—for example, a document, an e-mail, a meeting, or an oral presentation. But to get the product right, you need a good process, both to enhance your general communication skills and to solve specific communication problems. This chapter provides a brief overview of the management communication process; subsequent chapters provide detailed descriptions of each part of the process.

2

Process and Product

The management communication process (see the model on p. 4) aims to achieve an outcome that matches your goal. As you saw in Chapter 1, that goal could be to record some information, to inform someone of something, or—much more typically in management communication—to persuade someone to do something. Persuasion is the goal, for example, when you try to get someone to buy a product or service. You achieve your goal through a communication product—a sales presentation, which consists of words you both speak and write and visuals you show as you talk and include with your written proposal. That product is created through the management communication process.

That process is dynamic and, as you engage in it, probably appears seamless. But, like all processes, it comprises activities that can be isolated, studied, and practiced for improvement. The core activities of the management communication process are:

- *Analysis*
- *Design*
- *Creation*
- *Verification*

Analysis is at least half of the work and occurs before you write or speak. In it, you look at key variables: your intended outcome, your audience, the media in which you'll communicate, and the time when you'll communicate. Analysis leads to design, in which you solidify your choices about those key variables. The design phase in turn leads to the actual creation of the communication product. This product is the speech, memo, or report that you present to an audience. Before you actually present it, you have to verify the communication product, checking to see that it accomplishes what you intended.

In practice, as you write or speak, these phases seem to occur simultaneously—or even out of order. That's because you've been communicating all your life and have internalized the process so successfully that you don't separately identify and label all the activities but instead go through them unconsciously.

To make a sales presentation, you obviously prepare—you think about what you're going to say and how your audience will react. You gather information and arrange it. You put words on paper, or the screen, and then change them as you imagine how your audience will respond. You draft sections and move them around. You select effective graphs and pictures to support your arguments and think about where to place them within the overall presentation. You do a run-through, speaking to an empty room or to your colleagues to get feedback. You revise and try again, and as you do so you go back to the basics, rethinking what you're trying to achieve, how prepared your audience is, how effective your words and pictures may be for them, whether you're communicating at the right time to achieve the intended outcome.

As you do all that, you don't consciously say, "Now I'm analyzing," "Now I'm designing," "Now I'm creating," "Now I'm verifying." You just do it. But if you hit snags, or if you're working to improve your overall communication skills so you can write and speak with less anxiety and greater efficiency, it pays to think carefully about the process. Just as you perfect your golf or tennis by focusing on separate steps and then combining them into a single process, so when you communicate you focus on the four core activities of the management communication process. But recognize that they aren't necessarily sequential "steps" that you work through each time you write or speak. They are components of a dynamic process in which you move back and forth among analyzing, designing, creating, and verifying. Each component is briefly described below and discussed in more detail in the following chapters.

Analyze

Before you write or speak, you have to analyze the communication opportunity. Answer these four questions:

- *What* are you trying to accomplish?
- *Who* is your audience?
- *How* will you communicate?
- *When* will you communicate?

To answer these, you must focus on outcomes, think like your audience, select the best medium, and time your message appropriately.

- *Focus on outcomes.* Identify the outcomes you want from the audience—what you want the audience to know, feel, or do. You may have one or several outcomes in mind—for example, to inspire an employee to improve performance while at the same time expressing your support for what he or she is currently doing.
- *Think like your audience.* Analyze the audience(s) so you can see the issues from their point of view. Understand what they already know, what they want to know, how they feel about the issue you're communicating about, what they can do about it. The more you know about your audience, the more readily you can meet their needs and thereby achieve your goals.
- *Select the best medium.* Review the options for encoding your message and select the one with the highest likelihood of carrying the message effectively to the intended audience to achieve the intended goal. Options include written, oral, visual, and nonverbal media. Written and oral media can be formal or informal. Electronic media are increasingly available. Often, messages are best carried in multiple media, so you may select not a single medium but several—and make sure they work together.
- *Time your message.* Send your message at the right time. Communication often fails to achieve its intended outcome because it comes at the wrong time—when the receiver isn't ready to receive or can't act as you wish. There is no perfect time to communicate, but through careful analysis you can select the best time.

Design

When you have identified the intended outcomes, audience, media, and the right time for your message, you design the product that will address all these simultaneously. In doing so, schedule and prioritize your communication tasks and employ an interactive process to help you get your audience to be as receptive as possible before you actually deliver the product. Design the communication product to

- gain audience attention.
- provide the right information in the right sequence.
- make sure the audience doesn't get lost.
- make sure the audience understands and will comply.

Create

Create a communication product that *works*. For instance, create visuals and units of presentation timed to highlight and enhance oral presentations and briefings. Create visuals and units of text for print and online presentation including paragraphs, sentences, lists, and headings.

Verify

Verify that the communication product will, indeed, work. Test what you have written or prepared for presentation on three levels: effectiveness, efficiency, and conventionality. Be sure your final product incorporates the choices you made about outcomes, audience, media, and timing.

In the end, make sure the product bears a distinctive *brand*—your personal brand or that of your organization. An organization's brand represents business strategies aimed to develop worldwide recognition and the ownership of a market segment. Communication products should be instantly recognizable as *you* (the best you), in your role as an individual or as an organizational spokesperson. That brand—that distinctive voice and look—is the ultimate mark of trust between you and your audience.

SCENARIO

Sorting Out a Communication Assignment

The pressure Eloise Holtz felt at her current job was as intense as any she had experienced as an engineering student in her native Germany, as a management trainee at a French aerospace firm where she worked for three years, or as a student in the joint MBA–law degree program in California from which she had graduated a year earlier. After concentrating in international business law, Eloise joined the International Tax Advisory Services (ITAS) division of a large consulting firm, and the pressure she felt came from her assignment to make a presentation—something she had done dozens of times throughout her student days.

But the current situation was hardly academic. Eloise was part of a team of consultants in her firm, who were in turn working alongside a group of investment bankers. The two groups were jointly advising a large U.S. corporation on a merger it was pursuing with a European avionics company. A key issue in the proposed merger was the financial impact of differing treatments of tax issues between the United States and the European Union. The European firm in the proposed merger had itself made numerous acquisitions over the years and, as a consequence, carried a high level of goodwill and intangible assets on its balance sheet. Because the U.S. firm was offering a price significantly above the fair value of the acquired assets of the European firm, additional goodwill would be created in the deal. At issue was how the combined goodwill would affect the balance sheet of the new entity. Differences between E.U. and U.S. tax codes needed to be assessed to determine when and how the goodwill would be amortized and whether impaired assets would need to be written down. A recent pronouncement in the U.S. by the Financial Accounting Standards Board would allow the firm to avoid writing down goodwill each quarter as long as the assets were unimpaired. But because the ruling was new, its application was untested, and how it fit with E.U. standards was unclear.

As an expert in international taxation, Eloise felt confident in her ability to research the issues to arrive at reasonable estimates that the two merging firms could work with in projecting pro forma financial statements for their boards and investment bankers. She felt less confident about how to present her findings.

And time was tight. The head of ITAS told her on Friday that she would be giving her presentation that next Saturday in Paris to the two teams—ITAS and the investment bankers—and the CFOs and senior financial staffs of the merging companies. Before then, he wanted her to run through it on Tuesday in New York, then refine it before leaving for Paris on Thursday for another rehearsal, on Friday, with both ITAS and the investment bankers.

Eloise welcomed the chance to revise her presentation based on reactions from colleagues. But she was troubled by her manager's instruction to "keep it short and simple," giving "just the facts," "without all the fuss and bother of PowerPoint and that kind of stuff." A long-time consultant, he was not as comfortable with PowerPoint as Eloise and her peers had become through years of academic training. Eloise knew that her fellow ITAS consultants and the investment bankers would expect a polished presentation, and she suspected the CFOs and their staffs would, too. But the first person she had to satisfy was the head of the team, and when he urged simplicity she knew he was expecting a few overhead slides with key information that she would orally describe and explain.

Eloise was glad she had researched thoroughly and had in hand the information she needed for the presentation. She already had arrayed the data to show the balance sheet impact of three possible scenarios for tax treatment, depending on different tax codes and the change in U.S. accounting standards. That, it seemed, was simple—compared with how to put together her talk to satisfy potentially conflicting audience expectations and the need to meet three different deadlines in sequence. But at least she had the weekend to do the work. The question was where to begin.

Questions for Discussion

1. Where in the management communication process (analysis, design, creation, verification) do you think Eloise is as she faces a weekend of work? Does that seem to you like the right place for her to be?
2. Using the *what, who, how,* and *when* questions, analyze the communication situation. Does Eloise have answers for each of these now? What else does she need to know?
3. Sort out the three versions of the communication situation—the two run-throughs and the final presentation—and answer the *why, who, what,* and *when* questions. Are there differences among the three versions? If so, are they significant enough to cause her to change the focus or content of each version?

4. Should Eloise work through the four stages of the management communication process in sequence, or is there any advantage to beginning somewhere other than at the analysis stage? What might she gain or lose if she begins at another stage?
5. How should Eloise handle the conflict she senses between what the head of ITAS tells her and the way she thinks she should proceed? Specifically, what would you advise her to do about the informal instruction to avoid a PowerPoint presentation?
6. When the time comes to verify her presentation (or presentations), what standards should Eloise use? What can she do now to help make the verification stage easier and more effective later?

CHAPTER

Analyzing Outcomes and Audiences

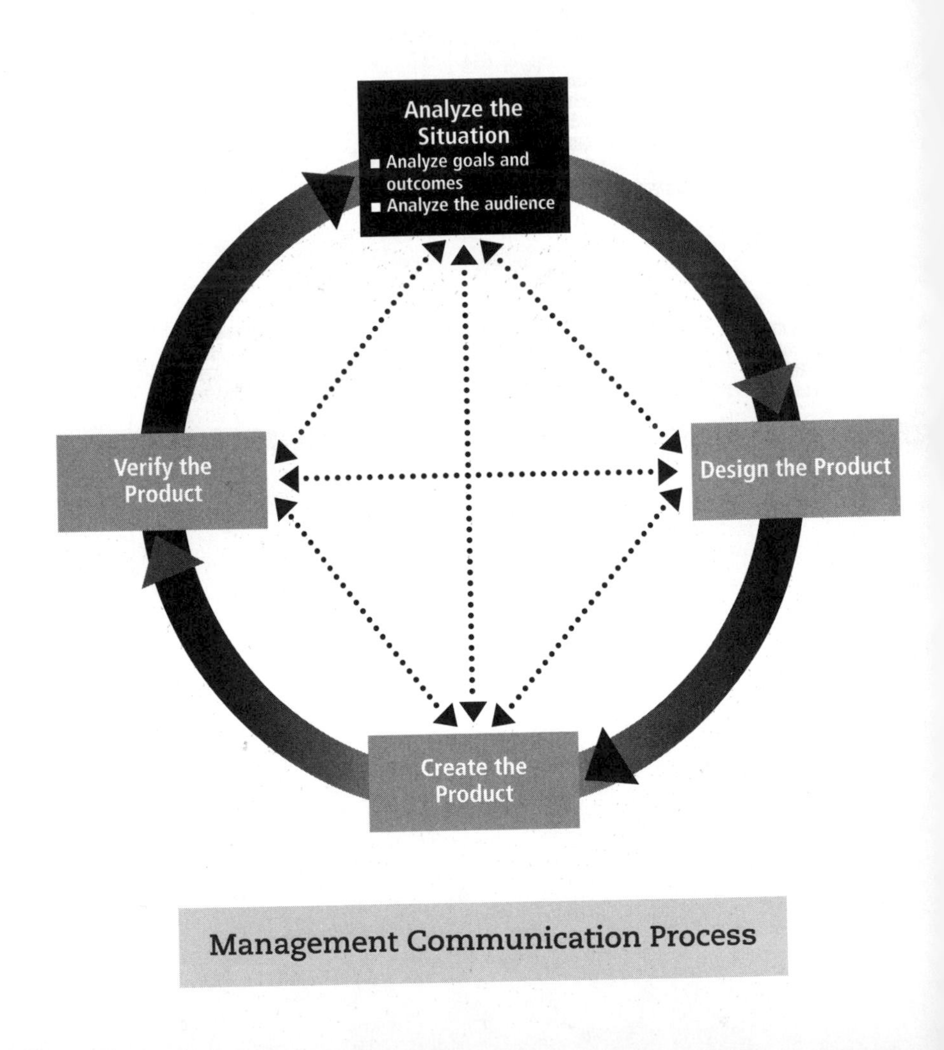

As a manager, you assess every situation before you act. Thoughtful analysis prevents problems and promotes efficiency. When you communicate as a manager, you analyze the specific communication situation you face, looking at outcomes, audience, medium, and timing. This chapter discusses the analysis of the first two of these variables: outcomes and audiences. Chapter 4 looks at media and timing.

3

Goals, Outcomes, and Audiences

Managers communicate with a purpose: to achieve an outcome in, with, or through someone else. You might

- write an e-mail to the human resources office confirming the hiring of a new administrative assistant in your department.
- report to the vice president for finance, orally and with a follow-up document, on your estimate of cash flow for the next three quarters.
- make a formal sales presentation to a potential buyer on the advantages of a new enterprise software program your company produces.

Each of these communications has a goal that can be achieved only by presenting information to someone else.

The communication model (see Chapter 1) helps identify the goal, outcome, and audience in each of these situations. In the first, the goal is to *record* that a new person has been hired. In the second, the goal is to *inform* the financial vice president about your cash-flow projections. In the third, the goal is to *persuade* the customer to buy the software. *Record, inform,* and *persuade* are generic, abstract terms. As you analyze a communication situation, you move to more concrete levels because it isn't enough to know that your goal is, say, persuasion. You identify the specific goal—in this example, to sell the new enterprise software. The success of your communication depends on focusing as concretely as possible on the goal.

Goals (what you want), *outcomes* (what you want someone else to know, feel, or do), and *audiences* (the person or persons with whom you are trying to achieve something) are thus closely linked elements in the management communication process. You need to think about them separately and together. Figure 3.1 presents some questions about goals and outcomes to help you begin your analysis.

Answer these questions to determine goals and outcomes:

What do you want to happen as a result of your communication?

Do you want to *record* information? *Inform* someone? *Persuade* someone?

Do you want your audience to *know* something? *Feel* something? *Do* something?

Can the audience do what you want? Is the audience *ready* and *able* to do what you want?

Figure 3.1 | Analyzing Goals and Outcomes

Single and Multiple Goals

Few management situations involve simple, single goals. Imagine that you are talking with an employee about his tardiness. The outcome you seek is to motivate him to get to work on time. But you have a second goal: to do so in a way that doesn't alienate him. That's an important aspect of the desired outcome because you want him to change his attitude and behavior. So you select your words carefully to highlight the point, but you also use phrases like "I know you want to be successful at this job" or "Your work is good, but you need to be at your desk at the times we agreed on." You moderate the message ("Get to work on time") in language that keeps the employee from tuning you out. You structure the message indirectly, leading to the main point (that he needs to be on time) after establishing common ground (your shared desire for his success).

Now imagine that the employee has been warned several times, and your goal is to fire him. You structure the message differently, putting the main point ("Your employment here is terminated") up front. A different goal also causes you to use different phrasing and a different tone. You consider the legal implications of your message and use language that will protect you and the company from a charge of unlawful discharge. You cite company policy, relate the employee's tardiness to specific job requirements, and avoid indirect language of the kind you selected when you were trying to motivate him toward better behavior.

In each situation, focus on the precise outcome you seek. Different outcomes require different words, different structures, and possibly different media (e.g., when you are warning him, you may do so orally, but when you discharge him, you also put the message in writing).

Understanding Goals as Outcomes

Be clear about the *outcome* you seek from the person or persons receiving your message. Focus on what you want the receiver to know, feel, or do. In our example of the employee's tardiness, notice two very different intentions: motivation or termination.

Which do you want? The answer helps you shape the communication product. If you can't distinguish between the two outcomes, your communication will fail because you will not be sending the employee a clear message. He may be left wondering if you really want to get rid of him, whereas you are in fact merely thinking you want him to be prompt in getting to work. Such ambivalence can cause serious conflict.

Think about your goal or goals from the point of view of the receiver of the message. You might guess that the employee wants to stay with the company and therefore wants to improve his behavior. That would lead you to emphasize one outcome improvement in the employee's behavior. But if you suspect that his tardiness is really a form of acting out—that he doesn't like the job and would be happy to be out of it but can't take the step of quitting—you shape a different communication product, one that reflects a different intended outcome—the employee's dismissal. In this instance, you might begin with questions rather than statements: "Are you happy here? Do our company hours conflict with some other needs in your life?" You would lead the employee to a recognition that he should work elsewhere.

Although you cannot know everything about everyone with whom you communicate, you can refine your communication goal by thinking about the outcome you desire. Doing that leads you to analyze the audience, the receiver in or through whom you seek that outcome.

Audiences

Management communication succeeds when the person or group that receives your message understands something they didn't understand before, or does what you want because you have convinced them that *they* want to do it. The more you know about those receivers, your audience, the more effectively you can tailor your message to achieve the intended outcome. Figure 3.2 presents some important questions about audiences.

Single and Multiple Audiences

Some on-the-job communications are intended for one known audience. Examples include a memo reporting on a business trip (though the expense report may be detached and forwarded to another office for payment); a phone call to the maintenance supervisor asking that the parking lot be plowed; a cover letter to a customer who wrote to request a copy of the user's manual for the software you sell.

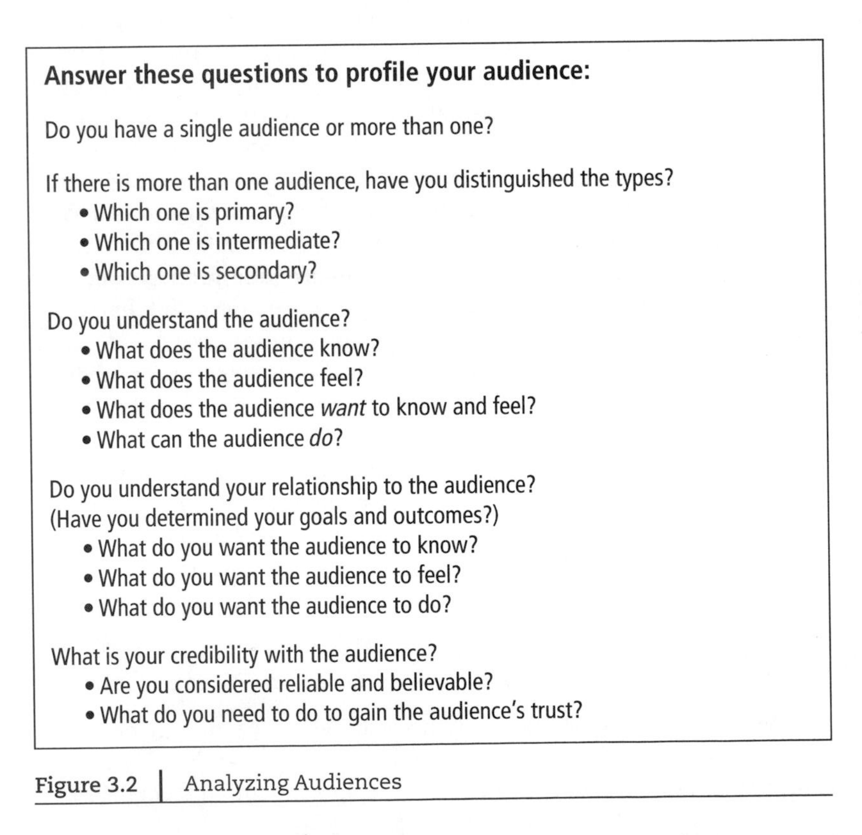

Answer these questions to profile your audience:

Do you have a single audience or more than one?

If there is more than one audience, have you distinguished the types?
- Which one is primary?
- Which one is intermediate?
- Which one is secondary?

Do you understand the audience?
- What does the audience know?
- What does the audience feel?
- What does the audience *want* to know and feel?
- What can the audience *do*?

Do you understand your relationship to the audience?
(Have you determined your goals and outcomes?)
- What do you want the audience to know?
- What do you want the audience to feel?
- What do you want the audience to do?

What is your credibility with the audience?
- Are you considered reliable and believable?
- What do you need to do to gain the audience's trust?

Figure 3.2 | Analyzing Audiences

Communicating with a single audience is generally easier than communicating with multiple audiences because you can tailor your product with precision. If you know that the manager to whom you're writing a trip report likes plenty of details, you can provide them, whereas if he prefers brevity, you can omit details. When you call the maintenance supervisor about the parking lot, you phrase your request based on what you know about that person: right to the point if that's what he likes, or roundabout, starting with a joke or a comment on the weather if that's appropriate. A single, known audience makes choices simpler.

More complicated—but far more typical—are business situations where you address multiple audiences. Here are two examples:

Example 1

As the information specialist in your company, you are assigned by the managing director to send a memo to 12 persons to explain a new policy on personal use of e-mail. You know that while some of them never use the company's system for personal messages, two send and receive more personal than business e-mail, and several others frequently use the system for personal messages. How do you begin? You might say, "Because personal use of the company's e-mail system interferes with business use, we are adopting a new policy." Will that offend the majority of the audience who never or rarely send personal messages? How detailed should your memo be? Can you cover every situation that might arise for everyone to whom you are writing? Should you go into technical matters like the amount of server memory consumed by storing graphics, or will that be not understood or considered irrelevant by the recipients?

As you prepare your memo, think consciously about the multiple audiences you are addressing and make choices—about tone, level of detail, word choice—appropriate to the fact that you are writing to more than one person. To accommodate the multiple perspectives of your audience, you might choose a neutral opening sentence: "This memo outlines the new policy on e-mail we are implementing to ensure efficient use of the system."

Example 2

You work for an investment banking firm and are writing a report assessing the investment potential of a new casino complex to be built on land owned by Native Americans.

The persons in your firm who will make the final decision about whether to commit capital to the project will read your report, but they will share its principal conclusions and recommendations with the casino's developer, who is seeking the investment, and he in turn will discuss it with the tribe on whose land the casino is to be built. Additionally, you know that residents near the tribal land are adamantly opposed to the project and intend to go to court to block it, so it's likely that your report will be obtained by them through the legal discovery process and may then be submitted to a court as part of their suit. At that point, your report will be on the public record and quoted in media stories about the controversy. The structure, tone, technical level, and words and graphics you use in the report must therefore be weighed in relation to all its potential readers and the different perspectives they have on the issue.

Types of Audiences

To sort out the multiple audiences in these examples and weigh their relative importance, distinguish among *types* of audiences (Figure 3.3):

- The *primary audience* is composed of the person or persons who can do what you want; they are the ones to whom the communication is directly addressed because it is through them you can achieve the outcome.
- The *intermediate audience* (also called *gatekeepers*) is composed of the person or persons who pass your communication to others.
- The *secondary audience* includes other persons who may also read or hear the communication and be affected by its message.

In our first example, the 12 staff members receiving your memo about the new policy are the *primary* audience, the ones who must understand the policy and act on it. The managing director who asked you to write the memo is the *gatekeeper,* because she will distribute it to the others. In this instance, there are no secondary audiences.

In the second example, the *primary* audience is the person who will

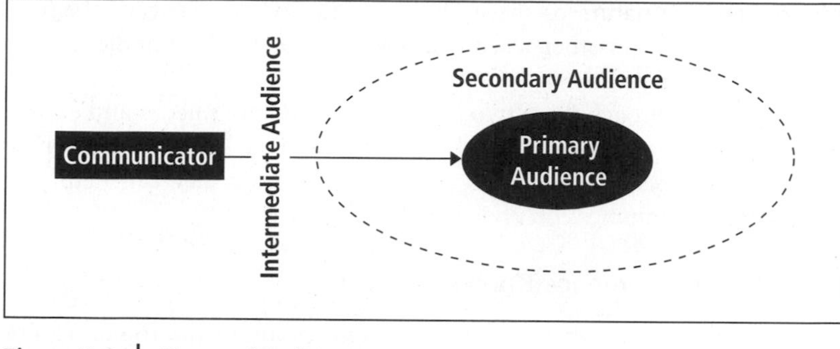

Figure 3.3 | Types of Audiences

make the final decision on whether to invest in the new casino. The decision maker may ultimately be one person or a group. As your report makes its way toward the decision-making body, one or several *gatekeepers* may read it and may ask for changes—for example, the vice president above you, the executive vice president to whom she reports, and then the president. The casino's developer, the Native American tribal authority, the opposing neighbors, the court, and the public may all become *secondary* readers—interested parties who will see what you write but who are not the direct, intended recipients.

Like most business situations, these audience considerations can become complex. Don't let the analysis cripple you. But do take time to analyze, pegging the amount of analysis to the significance (low to high stakes) and level of complexity (simple to complex) of the situation. In the first example, you merely need to keep in mind that someone will review the memo before it's sent and that its 12 recipients have varying needs and expectations. In the second example, the sensitivity of the situation and the high stakes of the final decision should lead you to explicit analysis of the many potential readers and the varied ways they could react to what you are writing. To get the job done in either case, you need to be aware without being overwhelmed.

Audience Needs—and Yours

The specific choices you make in preparing any communication product depend on the number and type of audience(s), but far more important is the nature of the audience(s) and what you want them to know, feel, or do—in other words, how you understand the audience and your relationship to them.

You can approach these two issues—the audience's needs and expectations and your relationship to the audience—by asking and answering the questions presented in Figure 3.2. Let's see how they can help you make smart communication choices.

What the Audience Knows and Feels

First, determine what the audience knows about the topic. You're aware that if you're writing for an audience of physicians to describe a new drug your company is marketing, you can expect a high level of technical knowledge and consequently use chemical and biological terms. However, in writing a letter to a layperson about the same drug, you would avoid technical terms and emphasize user benefits in simple language. Recognizing the audience's level of knowledge about a topic helps you select appropriate language and adopt a suitable pace for your presentation.

It's equally important to assess audience emotions—not just what the audience knows but also what it *feels*. Management communication deals overtly with knowledge, but audiences have emotions, and these need to be recognized and accommodated. If you're dealing with dissatisfied customers or unhappy employees, their level of knowledge is far less important than the feelings they exhibit. You write or speak accordingly, trying to put yourself in their position and respond to them as you would like to be responded to under similar conditions. If you're speaking to someone who's angry about the product you sold, it isn't helpful to begin with a technical description of its proper functioning. Instead, begin indirectly, acknowledging the anger, expressing your understanding of it, and then trying to move to the factual topic and a resolution of the problem.

Your Credibility with the Audience

Try also to gauge the audience's knowledge of and attitude toward *you*. Are you credible in their eyes? Credibility comes from two sources: you as an individual and as part of an organization and your communication product. Figure 3.4 presents examples of credibility from both sources.

The greater your own credibility, the less you may have to say to be convincing: a quick answer to a request may be enough if the audience is predisposed to trust you. You can reinforce your inherent credibility—and create credibility if your audience doesn't know you—by making the com-

What gives YOU credibility as a speaker or writer?

Authority
- What position do you occupy and what is your role within the organization?

Expertise
- How much knowledge do you have about the topic?

Track record
- How much experience do you have with the situation or with the audience?

What gives YOUR COMMUNICATION PRODUCT credibility?

Attractiveness
- How well is the written product designed?
- In a presentation, how appealing are the visuals, body language, speech?

Integrity
- Is the information complete, logical, and convincing?

Clarity
- Will the audience members learn what they need and comprehend what they read or hear?

Correctness
- Are there any errors in the content or expression?

Figure 3.4 | Sources of Credibility

munication product itself credible. When you assess your credibility with the audience, you spot strengths to use (e.g., your role as CEO, or your expert knowledge) and weaknesses to overcome (e.g., your relatively low organizational position, or your lack of detailed knowledge on the topic).

What the Audience Wants

As you shape a communication product, think about not just what your audience already knows and how it feels but also what it *wants* to know and feel. If a new client of your investment firm asks about tax-efficient ways to save for her grandson's college education, she doesn't want a lecture on capital markets. Determining what an audience wants to know often requires negotiation. You ask a question; she responds; you ask another; she provides further details. The feedback loop between receiver and sender (see the communication model in Chapter 1) provides a channel for refining her question so your answer fits it—that is, achieves the outcome. You are, in effect, teaching her how to ask the right questions.

Gauging what an audience wants to *feel* also requires some thought on your part before you begin. How many bad jokes have you heard from an after-dinner speaker who assumes his purpose is to make you laugh? After drinks and dinner, many people may instead welcome a short, simple talk that makes one pertinent point because what they seek is not entertainment but resolution—instead of listening to a stand-up routine, they want to go home. It's your job as a communicator to assess what your listeners or readers want to know and feel.

You also have to understand what the audience can *do*. If the person who asks about investments for her grandson's college education tells you she is gathering information for the boy's father, recognize that she isn't going to open the account herself. Your job is to provide information, and that requires a different approach, tone, and structure than you would use if you were attempting to convince her to open the account herself.

Communication problems often occur because the speaker or writer assumes the audience is able to do something it can't. Your message may be the right one in all other ways, but if it makes a request that the audience can't meet it will not be successful. Knowing what the audience you're addressing can—and cannot—do will help you shape your message and deliver it appropriately.

What *You* Want from the Audience

As you assess what your audience knows, feels, wants, and can do, remember to keep yourself in the picture, too. It's critically important that you know what *you want* the audience to know, feel, and do. In other words, you need to understand your own goals with respect to the audience—the outcome you desire. Answer the questions in Figure 3.2 as you plan your communication. You should be able to fill in the blanks in this sentence:

> I want the person reading my letter to know _____________, feel _____________, and do _____________.

For example, you could say, "I want the client to <u>know</u> about custodial and college savings accounts and their relative advantages and disadvantages, <u>feel</u> satisfied that I gave her detailed and accurate information, and be confident in telling her son so he'll consider opening an account and investing through me."

Thinking like the audience as you consider what you want it to know, feel, and do helps you meet its needs—and achieve your outcome.

SCENARIO

Matching the Message to the Audience

Ichikawa Matsusuke is the senior human resources (HR) officer of a multinational industrial-chemicals manufacturer based in Japan. The company has production or sales and marketing offices in Japan, the United States, Sweden, Spain, and France. Because of the wide variation in governmental policies among those nations on issues such as collective bargaining, benefits, and workplace rules, Ichikawa has always faced difficulties in implementing corporationwide HR policies. A recent sexual-harassment suit at the manufacturing facility in New Jersey cost the company a great deal in legal fees, an expensive out-of-court settlement, and bad local publicity affecting recruitment. Concerned about the prospects of additional problems, Ichikawa was directed to develop a corporation-wide policy against sexual harassment and to institute training programs for supervisory staff to learn and implement the policy.

His first step is to draft a memo to HR directors at each of the facilities in the five countries. The memo will outline a proposed sexual harassment policy based on U.S. law, because it sets the most detailed standards, and a suggested training program to be undertaken at each facility. The contents of the policy and the training program are essentially boilerplate provided by the company's lawyers and HR personnel in the U.S. Ichikawa's challenge is to shape the message effectively for a diverse audience with different points of view.

First, he identifies the types of audiences the memo must accommodate. The primary audience consists of the local HR directors. But it must be sent through the managing directors of each operation—gatekeepers who must read the document and pass it on—with support and authority—to the HR directors. The supervisory staff who must understand the policy and be trained to implement it represent a secondary audience because they will be given copies of Ichikawa's memo by the HR directors in preparation for the training.

Ichikawa knows that the level of knowledge, interest, experience, and readiness to act varies among the HR directors, who reflect cultural differences with respect to worker relations in general and especially with regard to sexual harassment issues. From his own experience in dealing with culturally based norms in the different countries, he knows that each local HR director will regard the policy and training program from a different perspective.

For example, he knows that the U.S. staff, because of the New Jersey suit and because of strong national and state laws, will be fully prepared to accept and act on the issue. Similarly, the tradition of gender equality in Sweden will make acceptance relatively easy there. Gender relationships in Japan are a different matter, and he particularly worries about Spain and France, where "Latin attitudes," although to some extent stereotypes, will have to be taken into account, along with strong union power stemming from those countries' socialist traditions.

In shaping his message, Ichikawa looks for common ground among the various recipients. He also keeps a strong focus on his goal—the outcome he wants from the audience. He needs to establish clearly the reason for the policy and training program. That reason must gain immediate acceptance from all the readers of the memo—the gatekeeping managing directors, the HR directors, and the supervisors. He decides not to touch on moral or social issues (the rightness of treating all workers appropriately) but instead to ground his argument in simple business necessity: the company must adopt a policy and train people in it because otherwise it risks serious financial penalties and bad publicity. He recognizes, though, that the strict business imperative will be better understood and accepted by Americans than the others since they have direct experience with the consequences of workplace harassment. He decides to address this difference by saying that the policy is based on U.S. standards simply because they are the highest and that local variations that fall short of those standards would make for administrative problems at the corporate level and might subject U.S. operations to legal challenge.

Although Ichikawa understands that local HR directors may still have varying levels of acceptance of the policy and program based on cultural differences, he wants to establish authority by using a directive, top-down tone that doesn't invite quibbles or questions. He uses a similarly direct, logical approach to laying out the policy and the training needed to implement it. Although Ichikawa is oriented to consensus and inclined toward building common ground through discussion, he understands that writing a memo that invites criticism and argument will not serve his purpose because of the varied nature of his audiences. This communication, he believes, calls for unambiguous expression and a commanding tone that leaves no room for doubt on the part of his audience.

Beyond the national and cultural differences Ichikawa recognizes among his audiences, he sees a common trait, partly the consequence of his Japanese company's own culture—to follow orders. He believes, therefore, that his appeal to authority will work, cutting across cultural differences to emphasize that the company expects adoption of the policy and implementation of the training program.

Questions for Discussion

1. How does Ichikawa try to think like his audience? What traits and characteristics of his varied audience does he emphasize? Are there others of equal or greater importance?
2. Does he focus clearly on his goal? Does he understand that goal as an outcome to achieve among those to whom he is writing?
3. Does Ichikawa know enough about the five HR directors to whom he's writing? What should he know about them, and how would that knowledge help him shape the message?
4. Does Ichikawa's appeal to authority seem appropriate to you? Or should he invoke other sources of credibility: his own standing with the audience? His specific technical knowledge? What are the advantages and disadvantages of employing multiple sources of credibility?
5. Does Ichikawa's reliance of his understanding of "national characteristics" (e.g., Latin attitudes toward women) constitute stereotyping or profiling? To what extent is stereotyping or profiling a necessary component of good audience analysis? When might it go too far?
6. Should Ichikawa put as much weight as he does on the "gatekeeper" audience, or should he instead focus solely on the primary audience?

CHAPTER

4

Analyzing Media and Timing

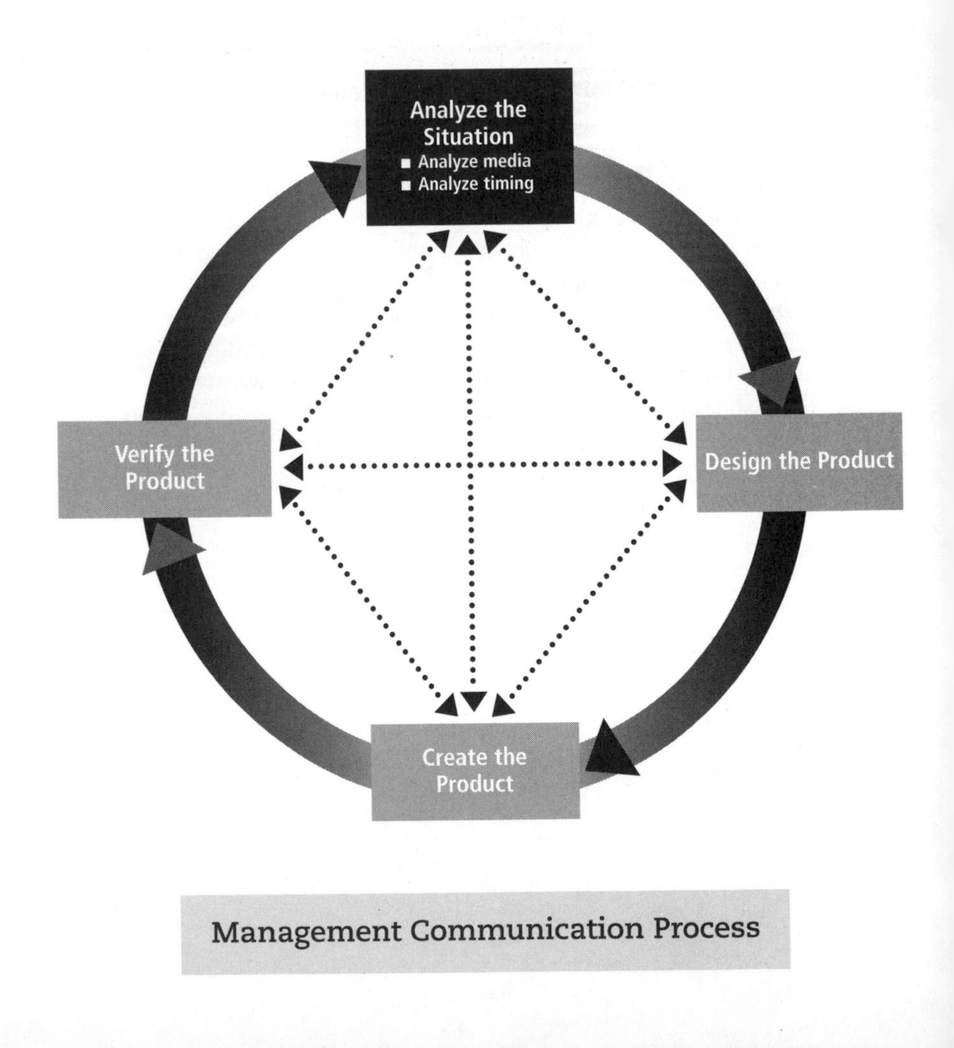

You've analyzed the communication situation to identify outcomes (*why* you're communicating) and audience (to *whom*). You also need to think also about *how* and *when* you'll communicate. Because the right message conveyed in the wrong medium or at the wrong time can fail to achieve your goal and meet your audience's need, you weigh your choices in communication *media* and *timing*. Like outcomes and audiences, media and timing are closely linked but can be separately analyzed.

Media for Communicating

The media for communicating business messages are varied and rich. Figure 4.1 groups these media into three categories (oral, written, and nonverbal) and shows some common business examples of each.

Oral media range from informal hallway conversations to formal presentations. They can occur between two persons or among many. They may be conducted in person or be mediated through technology (teleconferences and videoconferences).

Written media include visuals and text. They may stand alone but are often used together—for example, a written report may include both text and visuals. Written media may be sent either on paper or electronically.

MEDIUM	EXAMPLES
Oral	Conversation; question-and-answer session; phone call; teleconference; videoconference; meeting; informal and formal in-person presentation
Written (on paper or electronically)	**Visual:** Chart; graph; photograph; video; film; PowerPoint slide; Website **Text:** Hand-written notes; printed memo; letter; proposal; report; e-mail; PowerPoint slide; Website
Nonverbal	Body language (gestures, posture, clothing); voice

Figure 4.1 | Media for Management Communication

Nonverbal communication (see Chapter 7) comes into play with oral media: you use body language like gesturing, smiling, raising your voice, or arching an eyebrow to reinforce a point.

Media differ, too, according to the amount of feedback they offer. Conversations, for example, encourage rich, immediate feedback, whereas printed documents delay the feedback and make it formal and less interactive. (See pp. 38–39 for further discussion of negotiation through feedback.)

Matching Media

Although the variety of available media makes communication exciting, it also presents choices that can seem bewildering. Making smart choices requires you to match the medium to your intended outcome, the audience's needs and expectations, and the content of the message. You should also play to your own strengths by, if possible, using a medium with which you're comfortable and proficient.

Assess each situation according to:

- *The outcome you desire.* If you seek immediate action, a short oral message, delivered in person or by telephone, may be best. To create understanding on the part of the audience, you may choose a longer, written format such as a formal report.
- *The needs and expectations of the audience.* If the audience is familiar with the topic, you don't need to provide lengthy background in a formal report but might instead use a short memo that captures the key points and makes the central recommendation. If the audience is assembled for an oral presentation, you need to meet its expectations by delivering a fairly formal speech, probably with appropriate visuals and a written handout to summarize your point.
- *The content of the message.* A complex financial argument needs to be buttressed with tables and charts. An abstract topic (e.g., international trade) may not be fully captured in visuals but instead requires closely reasoned verbal arguments to deal with economics, politics, and legal structures. Some topics lend themselves to brevity (e.g., a quarterly P&L report), while others require elaboration (e.g., the adoption of new auditing standards).
- *Your strengths as a communicator.* Are you better at speaking than writing? Are you visually inclined? Are you better with words than

pictures? The primary determinants of the choice of media are the outcome, audience, and message, and if those dictate a medium with which you're less than comfortable, you simply have to rise to the occasion and do what's required. But if you have a choice—if you can select whether to make an oral presentation or submit a written report because both would be appropriate—then go the route that taps your skills and strengths.

The medium in which you deliver your message should reinforce rather than compete with it. Physicists recognize "noise-to-signal" ratios, and so should communicators. Reduce the noise so the signal comes through by selecting a medium that doesn't get in the way. Overly elaborate PowerPoint presentations, for example, are sometimes criticized for taking on a life of their own and detracting from the main job of getting the message to the audience.

Build In Redundancy

People vary in how they receive and process information. Visually oriented people like pictures, and text types prefer prose. Some understand better when explanations are oral, while others need to see the words in writing. An audience whose first language differs from yours will benefit from rich visuals that help transcend language barriers. Use different media to meet such differing needs—for example, presenting both text and visuals in a report or talk, and following up an oral presentation with a written summary.

Most people process best when they receive information more than once and in more than one medium. One large U.S. corporation follows what it calls "the rule of six" by aiming to deliver every key message to its employees six different times and in as many different media (e-mail, public presentations, one-on-one meetings) as possible. Such apparent redundancy allows the company to exploit both the effectiveness of repetition and the richness of media.

Converging Media

Especially because of developments in electronic communication, media are converging. Is a PowerPoint presentation written or graphic? Both—and also oral, because you comment on the slides as they appear, and nonverbal, too, because as you discuss the slides on the screen you use gestures and other body language.

Exploit the variety of media to enhance your message, meet your audience's needs, and achieve your goal. Think about the different effects words and pictures have on different audiences. Use multiple media to reinforce your message. Recognize that since the differences are not always sharp and fixed, the convergence of media offers additional tools—and requires additional awareness on your part.

Negotiation Through Feedback

The message you send is often reshaped as you negotiate with your audience. The feedback loop of the communication model (see Chapter 1) is visualized as linear, but in practice feedback is rarely so. Think of management communications as residing along a continuum from those in which there is little or no feedback and hence no reshaping, to those in which rich, dynamic feedback promotes active negotiation between the sender and receiver. Different media offer different opportunities for dynamic reshaping. Figure 4.2 represents this continuum.

When you write a letter to a customer who sent a letter of complaint, your communication does not benefit from the receiver's feedback. You write strictly in response to the original letter (a form of feedback in a larger organizational sense, to be sure). If the customer writes a follow-up letter responding to yours, that letter is a form of feedback that causes you to reshape your message. You can imagine a series of such letters between you and the customer, each a feedback loop requiring additional reshaping of the message. Although feedback exists in this illustration, it is relatively static and linear and may fail to resolve the complaint.

Suppose, instead, that the complaining customer calls you. This informal, oral medium introduces rich feedback leading directly to negotiated communication. She outlines her complaint. You respond, perhaps by asking some questions to help narrow the nature of her complaint. She

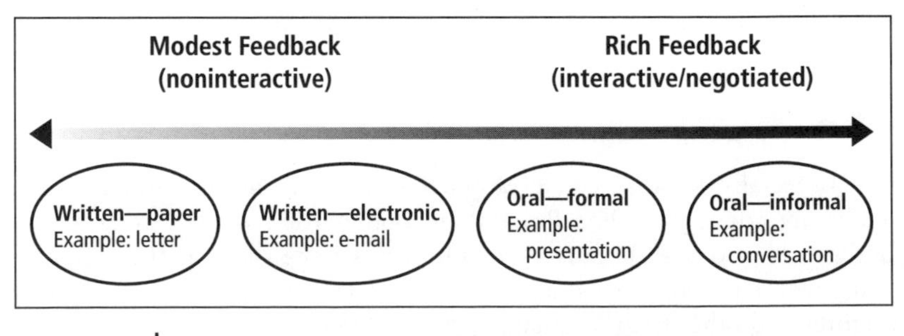

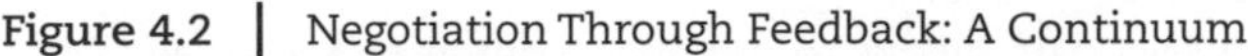

Figure 4.2 | Negotiation Through Feedback: A Continuum

provides additional details. You accept some and question others. She further refines her point. You offer a resolution. She expresses dissatisfaction. You select different words (or even a different message—for example, "We'll send you a refund"). Tones change—she grows angry because you sound unyielding, or you respond calmly to her anger and she adopts a similarly conciliatory tone. As the communication unfolds, you and the audience continue to negotiate by sending and receiving feedback.

The media in which you communicate offer varying levels of feedback and hence the opportunities for negotiation. Recognize these differences as you select the appropriate medium for your communication product. Choose media with rich feedback (e.g., conversation) when you need to engage the audience in shaping the message. Use media with less feedback (e.g., a letter) when the situation does not require negotiation.

Timing

As in life generally, in communication timing is critical. Decide *when* you should communicate as well as what you should say and how you should say it to a particular audience. Choosing the right moment is as important as choosing the right message or medium.

Finding the Best Time

Suppose you have a great idea for revising the purchase-order system your company uses. Do you catch your manager over the coffee machine and make your pitch? Or send a memo that he can read at his leisure? Or make an appointment to sit down with him and explain your idea? You may have good ideas about the new purchase-order system, but if you haven't really explored it in detail, thought through all the issues, and put the ideas together in a persuasive way, you should wait before making your case to the boss. Similarly, if he is busy, distracted by other matters, or not able to give you a full hearing, then you should delay.

Determine the best time to deliver your message by assessing the message, audience, and environment. Review the list of statements in Figure 4.3 and check "yes" or "no" after each one.

If you can answer "yes" to each, the time is right. If most of your answers are "no," the time is definitely not right. In most situations, you probably have a mix of positives and negatives. That's because there's almost never a *perfect* time to communicate. Sometimes you just have to

About Your Message	**Yes**	**No**
• I know the outcome I want.	☐	☐
• I know my audience and what it wants.	☐	☐
• I know the medium I'll use.	☐	☐
• I gathered and analyzed all relevant information.	☐	☐
• I organized the information appropriately.	☐	☐
• I feel confident about what I'm saying.	☐	☐
About Your Audience		
• The audience is ready to listen/read; they are not distracted.	☐	☐
• The audience is focused on the issue—or can become focused.	☐	☐
• The audience considers the issue important.	☐	☐
• The audience is able to act; they can do what I want.	☐	☐
About the Organizational Environment		
• My message fits the culture of the organization at this moment.	☐	☐
• My message builds on other ideas or messages in the organization.	☐	☐
• My message doesn't conflict with other ideas or messages in the organization.	☐	☐

Figure 4.3 | Timing the Message

move ahead, weighing the risks and taking responsibility if the communication fails because it's badly timed.

Although you can't expect perfect moments, you can seek the best ones by adjusting your communication strategies. Don't waste time on matters you can't change. This applies particularly to the organizational environment. If, for example, your company has just implemented a comprehensive energy-saving program that mandates the use of fuel-efficient automobiles, it would be the wrong time for you to propose the purchase of large luxury vehicles for the sales staff. That may seem obvious, but many people persist in lobbing memos and letters and e-mails into situations where prevailing corporate policy or the organizational culture makes their failure nearly certain.

In seeking the right moment for communicating, focus on those matters over which you have control. Principally, that means you and your message. If you defer communicating because you haven't gathered all the facts, haven't focused on an intended outcome, or don't quite know how you want to structure your argument, you know what you need to do. Your own work is under your control, and you can do that work to improve the timing of your communication.

Playing with the Clock

While you can't make a bad time perfect, you can take steps to improve the timing of your message. Here are some strategies for dealing with situations where the timing seems wrong.

Problem:
The audience is distracted, not ready to listen to you.

Solution:
Look for a better time. If you know the vice president to whom you want to make a pitch for increased staffing has to prepare for an all-day meeting with the CEO on Friday, don't bother to approach her until the following week. Don't allow your communication to fail because you insist on adding it to the existing pile of work your audience already has to contend with.

Problem:
The audience isn't focused on the issue or doesn't consider it important.

Solution:
Find a way to highlight the priority of your topic. If you have a cost-saving proposal, present it at the time when your manager is reviewing the budget. If you know the human resource director is preparing a presentation on benefits, your ideas about a flexible benefit program may be especially welcome. To show the importance of your project, to get attention for it, gather convincing evidence on why your idea is important and timely instead of simply assuming others already share your enthusiasm. Relate your interests to theirs, showing that the idea you have will help the audience solve a problem it has. Emphasize the benefits of your proposal to those receiving it. Look for common ground. Build sequentially, starting with an agreed point and working toward others that the audience may not have thought of.

Problem:
The audience can't do what you want.

Solution:
Determine just what the audience can do and tailor your message accordingly. For example, if the project you're interested in exceeds

the scope of your unit, you can identify that part of your project that does fit and attempt to sell it rather than the larger one. You can also use one audience as a gatekeeper who can pass your message to someone in the organization who is able to do what you want. For example, your immediate manager may not be able to approve your request for upgrading your department's servers, but if you make a good case he may direct it to the place in the organization where action can be taken.

SCENARIO

Weighing Media and Timing

Victor Santillo is the president of his family's apparel business in Mexico. The firm includes eight manufacturing facilities; most are simple sewing shops, but one is a new plant with highly sophisticated technology. The facilities operate under contracts with apparel companies from around the world who are attracted by relatively low costs and by NAFTA tariff advantages. Success for the family business depends on keeping the plants fully operational, a strategy that causes Victor to devote as much time to selling—to getting contracts—as to overseeing operations.

A Hong Kong company that markets high-fashion women's apparel has approached Victor about a possible contract. Although the family's business concentrates on mass-market jeans and shirts at its sewing shops, the Hong Kong firm is aware of the new plant's capacity to produce high-quality goods at competitive prices. The company's expression of interest comes in a faxed letter to Victor following a brief phone conversation. Because the letter lists specific questions (about costs, production rates, quality measures, and legal points), Victor knows that a phone response would be inadequate because of the amount of detailed information he has to convey. He could gather the requested information and send it by fax or e-mail. Either approach would be timely, and Victor wants to show his responsiveness, his ability to meet the customer's needs on their schedule. But he feels that such simple responses would not be effective in making his case.

As he sorts his options, he is aware that the message he wants to convey to the Hong Kong firm is twofold. Part of the message is quantitative and objective: the numbers asked for in the letter. But another part is qualitative and subjective: the "feel" Victor wants the apparel company to gain about the high-level production facilities. He wants to project the right tone and image, making a case for the capacity of his new plant to meet the high-fashion level of the clothing. The best way to do that, he reasons, is to have representatives of the Hong Kong firm tour the plant to see first hand its cleanliness and its computerized machinery. He also wants to present himself as a modern manager—the holder of an MBA from an American university as well as the head of a family business. But arranging a tour will obviously take time. Victor doesn't want to appear to be delaying.

He finally decides on an approach that involves several different communications. The first step is a phone call to the company in Hong Kong to thank them for their written request and to provide an overview of how he will respond. The personal touch, he knows, is important in the apparel business, especially with Asian businesspersons. In the conversation, he will outline how he will respond formally. First, he will fax a detailed response to the specific questions. Then he will invite representatives to come to Mexico to see the new facility and inspect some of the high-fashion clothing it is currently producing. After a tour of the plant—an opportunity for the company to see the facilities and also to interact with Victor at a professional level—he will make a formal presentation to the representatives, using PowerPoint slides to reiterate the quantitative data he will send first by fax and to reinforce the image he wants to project of a capable manager able to use high-tech equipment to produce high-quality clothing. Should the company reject his offer of a visit to Mexico, Victor is prepared to produce a video of the new facility to send them and also to set up a teleconference so he can make his pitch in a more personal way than a written response allows.

Questions for Discussion

1. What specific communication media does Victor select? Do they seem to you to be effective under the circumstances?
2. Does a mix of formal and informal media seem appropriate? Why or why not? What advantages and disadvantages does a mix of media entail?
3. How does Victor connect the two parts of his message to the media that he selects? That is, how does he enhance understanding and persuasion?

4. Does Victor time his multiple message appropriately—that is, to meet the needs of the audience and achieve his goal? What does he gain and/or lose by sending a series of messages at different times?
5. Does Victor rely on any national stereotypes as he prepares his response? If so, do these stereotypes influence his choice of media? How?
6. Does Victor's desire to highlight his management education contribute to or detract from the way he responds? Does his interest in doing so relate more to himself than to his audience?

CHAPTER 5

Designing the Communication Product

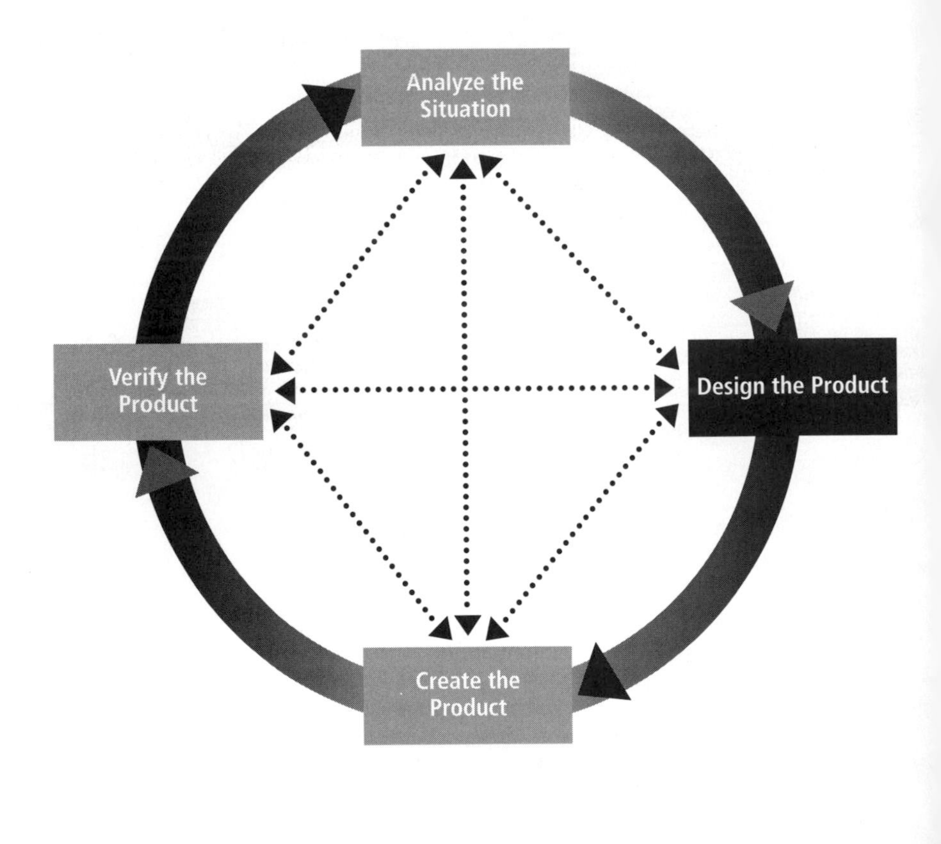

As you analyze the variables in the management communication process—outcomes, audience, media, and timing—your communication product begins to take shape (see Chapters 3 and 4). For an inevitable and uncomplicated communication task, like responding to routine requests for information, that analysis itself probably provides all the shape you need to create a message. Without further thought, you write an effective e-mail or make an effective comment in a meeting. The more complex the task and the higher the stakes in its outcome, however, the more you'll need to apply the strategies for designing outlined in this chapter.

Writing in Traffic

On most days, you probably manage several communication products in different stages of development. Like an air traffic controller, you need to schedule their arrivals and departures on your screen (see Figure 5.1). If you don't, as one observer noted, your life will become a miserable succession of emergencies. So create a plan of the *tasks* associated with your work. Chapters 10 and 11 describe strategies for planning collaborative endeavors that you can adapt for situations when you're writing on your own. Sort out the importance of each communication situation and respond appropriately.

Especially when the situation is complex, determine whether you should go ahead with the message, postpone it, hand it off to another person, or abandon it. The difficulty of your task alone should not drive your decision. Instead, ask questions like these:

- Is there a compelling reason to write or speak?
- Could the situation resolve itself without any communication?
- Is it more likely to resolve itself without any communication?
- Should the message come from me—or is someone else more likely to gain the audience's attention?
- Are there disadvantages to creating a written record?
- Would it be better to speak with the audience than write to them?

Sometimes, deciding not to communicate is the smart choice. In addition, recognize that not all communication products require the same level of effort or the same degree of polish. It's probably inefficient, for example, to spend time on the niceties of style in a routine update to project

Guidelines for Writing in Traffic

Establish or follow deadlines closely.

Set intermediate deadlines in advance of ones set for you.

Rank your tasks frequently to reflect new requests that take priority over current ones.

Sort your e-mail and voice mail messages into those that require immediate attention and those that can wait.

For lower-priority requests, **reply briefly** by noting receipt of the message and a time frame for your more detailed response.

Write long documents in modules to avoid being overwhelmed by length.

Limit the time you spend on writing (say, two hours), concentrate, then take a break.

Stop writing only when you know what your next module will be.

Print out your drafts from time to time to see how your argument is developing; it's often hard to get a sense of the whole when you work from screen to screen.

Separate writing and editing; look back as you write only to make sure you're on track, not to focus on surface details like word choice or sentence structure.

In an electronic notepad or on paper, **jot reminders** about where you are in a project so that you can get up to speed quickly when you return to work on it.

Figure 5.1 | Guidelines for Writing in Traffic

teammates. It is decidedly right, however, to compose with care the slides for a presentation to a major client.

Getting Attention

The care you take in composing presentation slides recognizes a condition pointed out by researcher Michael Goldhaber, among others: we live increasingly in an *economy of attention*. The scarce resource in management is no longer information, which now exists in abundance. Instead, it's knowing what information to pay attention to and cultivating in your audience the ability and willingness to hear or read your message. Plan your communication product to achieve that goal.

In general, people pay attention when

- *the writer or speaker is someone they trust:* in some cultures or situations, this means *experts;* in others, it means *family* or *long-term friends;* in others, it means *celebrities.*
- *they are shown the benefits of giving their attention*—for example, when the message helps them perform a task, solve or avoid a problem, advance a career, or feel better.
- *they are shown the risk of not paying attention*—for example, in cautions about strict compliance with organizational policies or the adverse effects of behaviors on health or longevity.
- *they are shown to be on common ground* with the writer or speaker.
- *the topic of the message is a hot one,* something the audience has been thinking about.
- *the writer or speaker makes it easy* for them to agree or comply.
- *the message is well designed*—aesthetically pleasing and eye-catching.

Developing Buy-In

To determine what will attract your audience's attention in a specific situation, consider talking with them while you develop your design. A conversation or two can reveal the audience's level of interest in what you have to say and suggest strategies for creating interest if the level is low. A good talk can also uncover gaps or wrong turns in your intended approach. You'll find it's much easier to make changes before you commit yourself to text and thus solidify what could turn out to be the wrong argument.

Talk, for example, about the *medium* (see Chapter 4) of the communication product. You have an increasingly wide choice, and that choice helps determine the structure and content of your message. You can't say as much in an e-mail as in a written report, but a brief e-mail may be all that's needed. You may also decide on more than one medium—for example, a short oral presentation with backup slides or an e-mail overview of a situation with attachments, perhaps with links to Websites for more extensive discussion. The audience's answers concerning media will give you a good idea about the extent and formality of the expected product.

In addition, be aware of any intermediate audiences between you and the intended reader or listener and ask about secondary audiences who may want to review the product (see Chapter 3). When you test presentation strategies with the intended audience and then incorporate their suggestions and comments in your design, you'll encourage the audience to buy into your message and comply with any request you may make. The audience will see themselves in what you have written or said, and most audiences in that position will like what they see.

To the degree that your audience does not share your values, discipline, culture, or language, such conversations can help negotiate agreement on the protocols of presentation. Avoid simply imposing your way of doing things. Instead, ask about preferences. Do they want a summary first? Do they like messages embedded in stories? Do they want an extensive description of the situation for the message and theoretical concerns—or do they find such elaboration of background tiresome? Explore a variety of options for structuring content, as this chapter suggests, and adjust your approach accordingly.

Brainstorming

In addition to talking with your audience to find what will draw their attention, talk with colleagues. Enlist someone who can listen to your thoughts and aid you in sorting through them. Often, that oral explanation itself will help you see where you are going, even if the colleague does nothing more than listen. Thinking out loud, too, helps you break though any barriers that might be raised by the idea of writing, a condition one MBA student refers to as "thesis paresis"—writing paralysis.

To foster creativity in such discussions, incorporate the strategies of thinking by association known as *brainstorming* (see Figure 5.2). Brainstorming is particularly suited to teamwork, but it may also be appropriate when you're writing something essentially on your own.

First, tease out key words that stand for your content; one word will often suggest another. Write each term on a sticky note (to make it easy to move them around in various arrangements) or on a blackboard or sheet of paper. In doing so,

- write quickly.
- write every term that anyone suggests or that suggests itself, no matter how seemingly far-fetched.
- don't judge the relevance or importance of a term: all ideas are equal.
- give yourself or your group a time-limit (say, 15 minutes) and take a break.

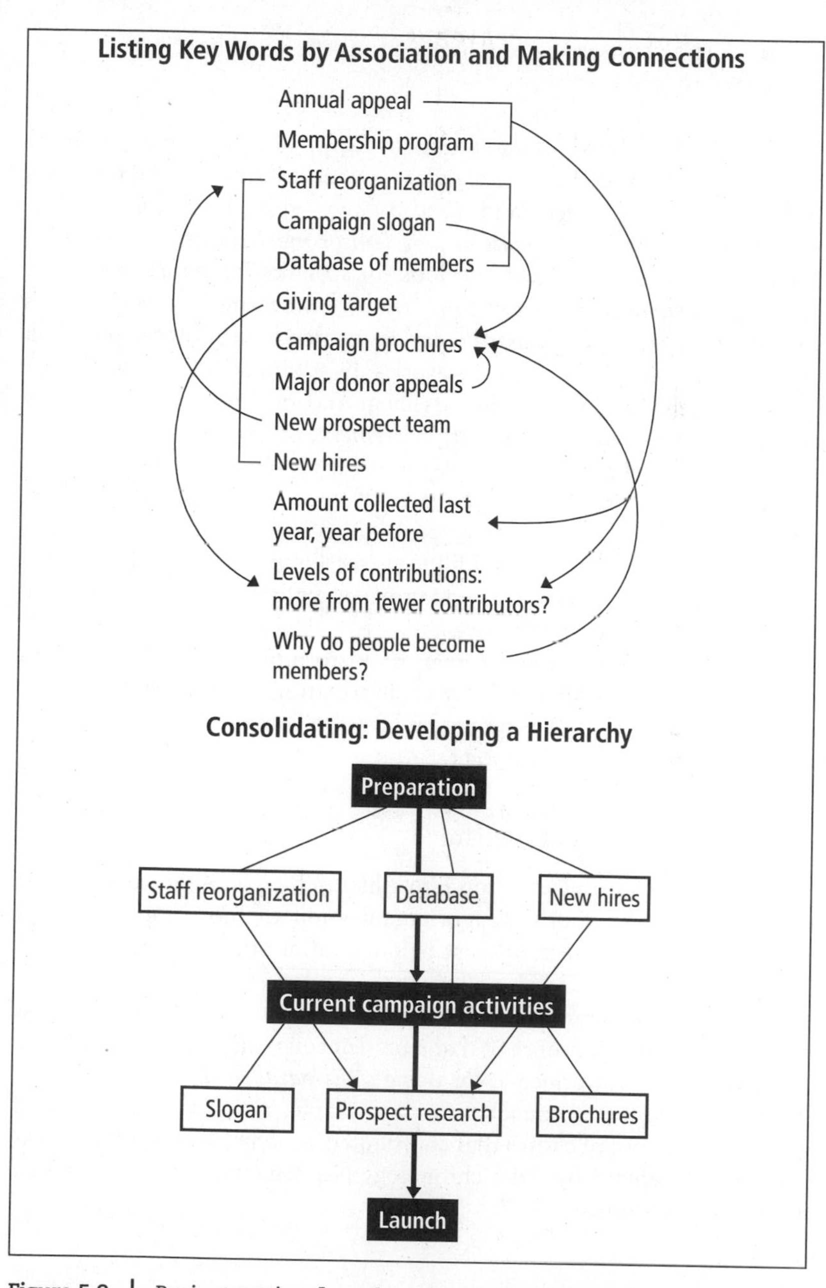

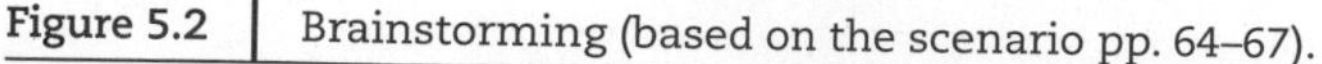

Figure 5.2 | Brainstorming (based on the scenario pp. 64–67).

- resume your session for a limited time until you have a good selection of terms.

Next, sort those terms into groups by identifying the common element that brings them together. Use standard higher-level terms, like *problems* and *solutions, advantages* and *disadvantages, reasons for and against, steps in a process, components of a system or mechanism,* a progression from *past* to *present* to *future.* Or look for specifics *(preparation, current campaign activities).* For example, a team brainstorming a new benefits package at its corporation listed every designated benefit they could think of and then came up with four categories (in addition to an "other" category for items like tuition reimbursement and membership in company clubs): *medical/dental* (the biggest), *retirement, insurance,* and *vacation.*

Finally, develop a visual display that shows relationships among the levels of your information (Figure 5.2). If your brainstorming seeks explicitly to find the causes of some problem, consider beginning your discussions with a blank map and fill it in (see Figure 5.3). The blank map prompts you to consider causes and provides a place to indicate and show relationships among those causes.

However you represent it, your brainstorming has two interrelated goals. You establish the hierarchy of information to be presented in the communication product. And you reduce the complexity of your information to its gist, to a main point.

Hierarchy and Parallelism

When you sort information into a hierarchy, you indicate that some elements of a concept or system or organization are more important than others, encompass others, or come before or after others (Figure 5.4). You sort your content into levels and show their relationship.

Within that hierarchy, however, you also identify elements that are at the same level of significance or that represent equal divisions of some larger item. The structural principle for doing so is *parallelism* (see Figure 5.5). Parallelism reinforces equality in, for example, a set of steps, a set of guidelines, a series of causes that contributed equally to a result, or an explanation organized by strict chronology (see Chapter 6 for more about parallel expression).

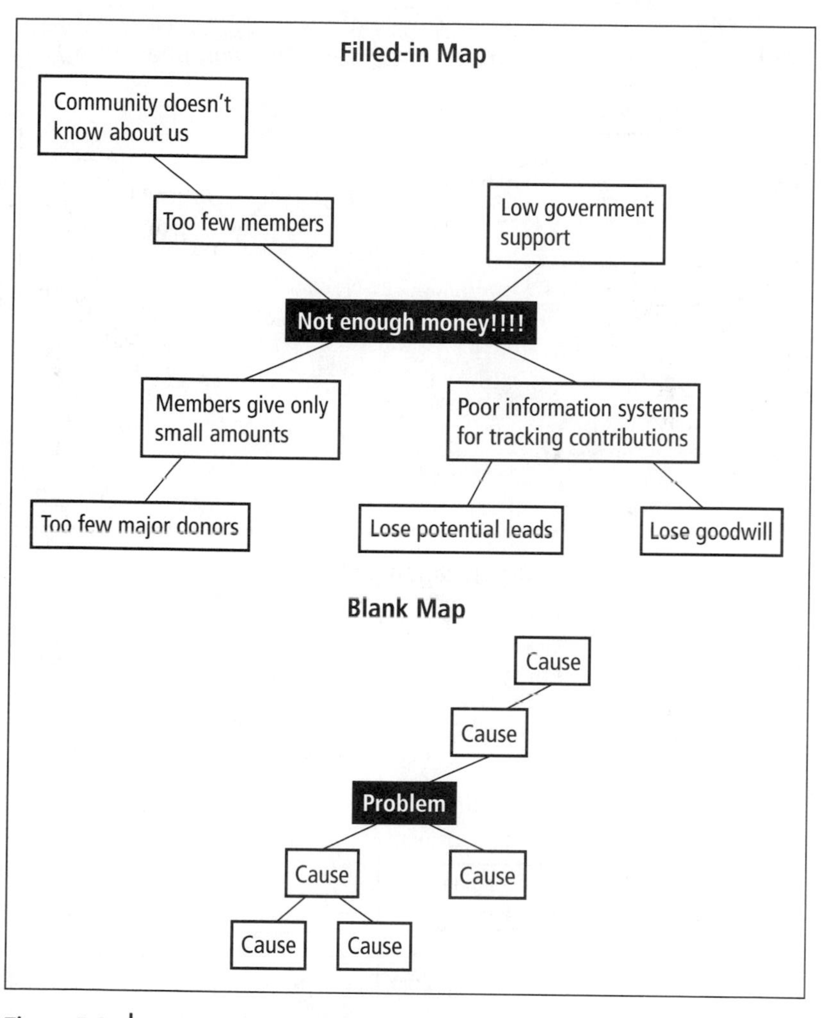

Figure 5.3 | Mapping a Brainstorm: The Causes of a Problem (based on the scenario pp. 64–67)

Main Point

Organizing your information into levels helps you compose a statement that brings everything together. That statement also reflects your sense of what will draw the audience's attention. If you can phrase your message as a "sound bite," you're on the right track.

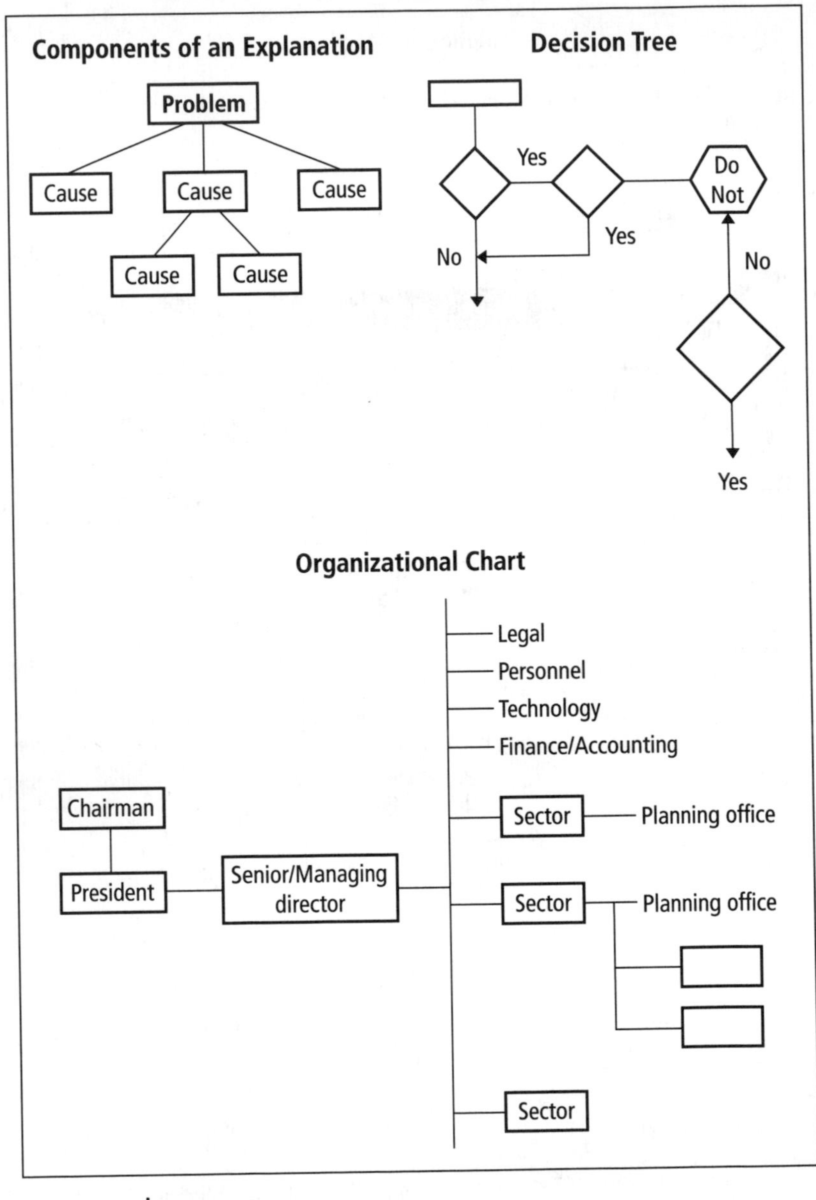

Figure 5.4 | Hierarchy

PROCESS	NARRATIVE		SPACE
Step 1	This happened	Monday	North side
	and then		South side
Step 2	This happened	Tuesday	East side
	and then		West side
Step 3	This happened	Wednesday	
	and then		Top
Step 4	This happened	Thursday	Bottom
	and then		
	This happened	Friday	Right
			Left

Figure 5.5 | Parallelism

Use the statement to

- summarize or explain your information.
- point out why this message is significant for the audience, now.
- forecast what will come in the communication product.

One statement may perform one or all of these functions. For example, a brainstorming session about the causes of increased first-quarter profitability at a retailer led to this explanatory sentence:

> Our increase in profits this quarter reflects two conditions that differ from those in the prior-year period: warmer winter temperatures and the occurrence of Easter within the quarter.

The report that followed treated each of those conditions as parallel and equal causes and discussed them in the order stated. A memo to staff accountants about new tax preparation procedures points out the significance and currency of the message and its implications for the audience:

> New IRS regulations require us to change our tax preparation procedures in ways detailed in the guidelines attached to this memo.

This opening alerts readers of the memo to the regulatory change and to their need to adapt their work accordingly. It also forecasts the guidelines in the attachment.

Using the Appropriate Genre

Because new situations for communication in organizations and industries frequently resemble situations you or others have faced before—for example, explaining company earnings or updating company procedures—you can often gain audience attention by using a communication structure from the known situation to fit the new situation. Such structures are called *genres,* templates for selecting and ordering information in a variety of recurrent circumstances. You're certainly familiar with the templates embedded in the software you use for writing, including the writing that supports oral presentations like PowerPoint. In addition, at a more complex level, genres reflect the knowledge about how to communicate developed by a community of practitioners in your organization or industry. Evoking the conventions of a particular genre with an audience who expects that genre gains the audience's attention.

One mark of your expert knowledge as a manager is an expanding repertoire of such genres. As researchers Yates and Orlikowski have shown, that repertoire often reflects a system of interrelated genres aimed to accomplish an organizational goal (see, for example, "Genre Systems: Structuring Interaction through Communicative Norms," *The Journal of Business Communication,* January 2002, 13–35). One genre system accompanies a sales or research and development project: request for proposal, proposal, progress report, final report (see Chapter 8). Other genres accompany the employment process: position description, letter of application, resume, letter of response to application, letter of recommendation, letter offering (or not) employment, contract letter (Figure 5.6).

A simple template or a set of genre conventions can be excellent starting places as you structure your content. They may also help you finish your communication product if you think they adequately fit your needs. If there are special twists to the situation at hand, however, you may play with the template or conventions to develop a more strategic approach. You don't *have* to use one of the slide formats in PowerPoint. In addition, be ready to change your approach as genres change. They change over time as

Outcome

- What is the outcome you are seeking?

  The genre signals the outcome. For example, a letter of application and resume *mean* that the writer is seeking a job from the audience.

Audience

- Who is your audience?

  The genre matches the mental model or expectations of the audience, and thus the audience can access information rapidly—as in the fact-sheet format of a resume rather than a narrative biography.

Medium

- What is the communication medium being used?

  For example, a former employer's comments in a telephone conversation with a potential employer about a job candidate may differ, even considerably, from comments the former employer would provide in a letter.

Timing

- What are the timing requirements?

  The genre system triggers the timing of requests and responses in communication products. For example, the deadlines in a request for proposal determine the timing for the writing of a proposal, for the selection of the winning proposal, for the awarding of a contract, and for the schedule of the project itself.

Figure 5.6 | Analyzing the Management Communication Process in Terms of the Appropriate Genre

- communities of practice change.
- technology changes.
- local norms yield to international needs.

Adjusting to New Practices

Genre conventions tend to develop locally within specific organizations or communities. You're probably familiar with forms and formats for task-related communication in your organization, structures that guide such routine documents as trip reports, periodic updates on sales or other activities, performance evaluations, purchase orders, and the like. Similarly, certain occasions for oral presentations may evoke standard structures: the five-minute Monday morning report to the executive committee, the team sales presentation to potential clients. Industry groups and professional organizations also develop guidelines—for example, international shippers use similar formats for letters of credit and accountants use similar formats for audit reports. As tasks and management change, however, the genres for accomplishing those tasks and informing management and clients need to change. But writers are often slow in reflecting those changes. Alert practitioners need to recognize gaps between the reporting tool and the work it should accomplish and adjust genre conventions accordingly.

Incorporating New Technology

A major force creating that gap is technology. E-mail, for example, has erased some of the distinctions between memos and letters and introduced into a written medium approaches more like talking. But e-mail is not all talk and not only an informal medium. When you're addressing friends, teammates, and, some studies show, people who work for you, the casual approach common to most e-mail is effective. But when you are addressing strangers, particularly those in another culture, clients, or executives, you need to adopt a more formal design.

In addition to e-mail, technology has fostered such new *interactive* genres as the chat room, the discussion box for commenting on drafts in online collaborative authoring (see Chapter 11), and, most significant perhaps, the Website. Website conventions are only gradually emerging. Most sites, for example, now include menu bars, usually on the left side of the homepage; graphics and color; and at least modest (sometimes extensive) use of multimedia presentation, including animation and videos. Although you may not design a Website yourself, you should be aware of the conventions and, in particular, of the need to structure the site for interactivity. Your site may be sequenced in one way; your reader may access it and arrange its components in another. In addition, consider visitors to your site more like users than readers. Especially on commercial sites, they want to *do* something, not just read. So you need to make it easy and speedy for them to act. For example, for readers who dip in and out of the site, sign each page (so they know who you are) and foster easy navigation, including a return to the homepage.

Addressing Global Audiences

Unless they are on a corporate or an organizational intranet, Websites address the world. And that increasingly global economy is another force for changes in genres. Proposals are a good example. Within a U.S. context, a written proposal offering to provide goods or services is a common document that, when accepted, becomes a binding contract. In less legalistic settings, however, such agreements may be arrived at only through discussion and confirmed without the creation of a document. In that case, international negotiators have to agree not only on the offer but also on the kind of communication product that each side's organization can accept as proof that the offer has been made and agreed to. Similarly, filings for the approval of new drugs have differed widely from country to country and regulatory agency to regulatory agency. Those differences slow the process of getting drugs to market and to patients. As the industry becomes increasingly international, the delays have become increasingly costly. In response, a committee of industry representatives is working on a common protocol, a common *genre,* for documentation that will work across the globe.

Developing Modules

When you brainstorm or use the conventions of a genre, you develop *modules* of content. Dividing what you have to say into modules helps your audience pay attention because it gives them one manageable component of an explanation or an argument to process at a time. It keeps them from being overwhelmed. A module may be a paragraph or a section. In a Website, those modules are relatively independent, tied by topic to a menu on the homepage. In a document or talk, which has a more linear structure, you need to develop not only the modules themselves but also a strategy for aligning them. In doing so, you make a series of moves through which you bring the audience from not knowing something to knowing something, from neutrality (maybe even opposition) to compliance. Broadly speaking, at least in the European tradition, these moves fit within a three-part pattern: introduction (or opening), middle, ending (see Figure 5.7). Your choice of a genre will dictate some of these moves. For example, here are typical moves in a letter of application for a job:

- *Introductory module:* how you found out about the company or job; what you are applying for
- *Middle module:* how you fit or exceed the criteria listed in the job description, usually in terms of education and experience (one or two paragraphs)

Introduction

- Engage the audience's attention.
- Set the scene: provide the context for this communication.
- Create urgency: note the purpose of your communication, the problem or request that necessitates this communication, now.
- State the main point and forecast the communication.

Middle

- Deliver the information you promised in modules that fit the framework you forecast.

Ending

- Provide closure.
- Remind the audience of your main point.
- Recommend future action, if appropriate.
- Tie up any loose ends while avoiding any new topics.

Figure 5.7 | Traditional Moves in a Communication Product

- *Ending module:* what's next: request for an interview, reference to enclosed resume, reaffirmation of your interest in the job.

Designing in modules helps the audience read. It also helps you write communication products because you can complete one module at a time, writing what you know best before writing tougher sections, gaining traction, for example, in some straight description while you await inspiration for the introduction.

Designing for Access

In the end, your design has to pass this test: what the audience most needs must be most accessible to the audience. To provide easy access,

- place the main point up front.
- make the structure of the modules explicit.
- incorporate *advance organizers,* textual or visual signals about what's to come.

Open with the Main Point

As one frustrated manager noted in response to the draft of a report that piled on details before coming to an important conclusion, "Why not just *tell me?*" Retracing your days on the road may be a suitable approach for your own sales log. But that narrative is much less suitable for an audience who has paid you for an answer, not a story. Instead of rehearsing the process by which you came up with your point, *start* with that point as you reorient information to the reader. If you expect resistance to that point, or to you, consider opening with background arguments to soften that resistance. In some cultural settings, too, a blunt introduction may be considered offensive. If so, be less direct: talk about the setting, or the weather, or your relationship with the people you are addressing. But most of the time, for most managerial communication, cut to the quick.

Make the Structure Explicit

Second, make the structure for your presentation explicit and forecast that structure in the introduction. Even informally, give an overview before you give details:

> Here are the answers to the questions you asked this morning, in the order in which you asked them.

In more formal presentations, you'll announce the structure—in a table of contents for a report, in an opening slide that lists the topics you'll cover in a talk, or in a statement at the end of an introductory section that details issues to be addressed and the order in which they'll be addressed in the remainder of the document:

> Our highly competitive benefits package is designed to achieve four important goals for our company, each of which is discussed in this report: maintain morale, reduce turnover, reward longevity, and control costs.

Use Advance Organizers

Third, within the document or talk, build in *advance organizers* that signal readers about what's to come and aid skimming and searching. The structure statement on the benefits package provides four advance organizers: "maintain morale," "reduce turnover," "reward longevity," "control costs." These become headings for each of the four modules that follow.

Use topic sentences to start paragraphs (see Chapter 6). Use such visual devices as a flow chart with boxes drawn for modules of an entire presentation; before each new module, reproduce the chart, in a document or presentation, with that module highlighted. Chapter 6 provides more details about these text devices as well as design strategies to foster access and readability on a page or a screen. Such devices only work, however, if the underlying structure is effective.

Outlining

To make that structure something you can *see,* develop an outline. Use the map of your brainstorm, although you may need to convert it from something only you can understand to a linear arrangement for presenting your information to others (see Figures 5.2 and 5.3). Traditional outlines use numbers or letters to label the levels of information:

I.
  A.
    1.
    2.

Or:

1.0
  1.1
    1.1.1

But indention alone may be enough to help you visualize the structure. The goal is to provide a snapshot of how the modules in your communication product relate to one another and to the main point, something you might want to write at the top (see Figure 5.8).

Unless you're asked to provide an outline that works for audiences other than yourself or your teammates, the form is up to you. It's your organizational tool. Include, for example, marks in the margin to indicate where you think some visuals might be needed.

If visuals, rather than text, form the core modules for your communication, as in the slides that accompany an oral presentation, you may outline as a form of *storyboarding.* Draw a thumbnail sketch of each vi-

Main Point

After eight months of preparation, the museum will launch its fundraising campaign under the slogan "Give today—grow tomorrow."

Outline

Preparation
- Staff reorganization (visuals: old and new organizational chart)
- Database

Current campaign activities
- Slogan (visual: logo)
- Prospect research
- Brochures

Schedule
- Launch activities (in table plus introductory text)

Figure 5.8 | Outline with Notes (based on the scenario pp. 64–67)

sual and then jot down some comments about it to spark your further discussion (see Figure 5.9).

The headings in your outline may represent standard headings in the genre (for example, in a resume: *education, experience, skills, personal,* among others). They may come from the audience's explicit request, as in a request for a proposal, that dictates the structure of a response. As you've seen, they may also pull key words from the sentence that expresses your main point (for more about headings, see Chapter 6).

When you write as a team, an outline is critical. Knowing the whole picture, each person can write modules separately and fit them together seamlessly at the end (see Chapter 10). The outline also helps when you go back to *verify* that what you wrote or said works. It's the standard against which you check a final draft or the run-through of a presentation (see Chapter 9).

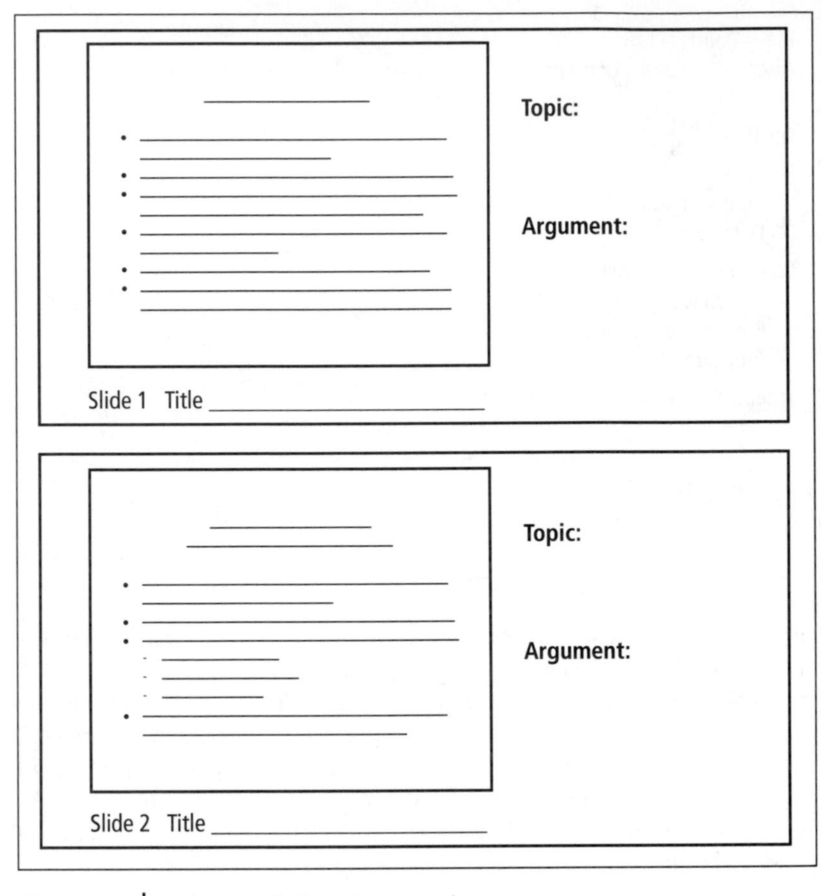

Figure 5.9 | Storyboards for a Presentation

SCENARIO

Designing a Report

After working for two years in fundraising for an American museum, Peter Townsend returned to his native London to accept the newly created position of manager of development for a large art museum. Because private support for the arts was a relatively new concept in the U.K., Peter's

American experience was highly valued by the museum as it prepared for its first large-scale fundraising campaign.

Eight months into the job, Peter was stopped in the hallway by the museum's director. "Need to put together my report for the Trustees, Peter," he said. "Appreciate a few lines from you—what you've been up to, where we stand, that sort of thing. A few pages will do. Need it in two days, sorry to say. Rush, rush, you know, like in the States."

Despite the casual nature of the request, Peter was pleased to have a chance to report on what he had been doing. Through reorganization and some hiring, he had been working hard to transform a small department oriented to a modest annual appeal and membership program into an organization capable of raising substantial funds through major gifts. But he wasn't sure where to begin to write the report. He realized that whatever he wrote would be incorporated, in some form, in the director's report, so the trustees of the museum would be the final audience. Having a chance to update the director was welcome. But did he really mean "a few pages"? It would be hard to explain what he had done for the past eight months in such a limited space.

Peter considered the director a bit distracted and more interested in exhibits than in fundraising. Still, he decided he needed to sit down with him and clarify exactly what the report was supposed to do. Peter managed to get a late-afternoon appointment to see him. To prepare, he made a list of the items he thought he should cover:

- results to date of the annual appeal
- current status of the membership program
- reorganization of the staff (new hires in membership and information systems, reassignments to emphasize fundraising duties for others)
- introduction of a computerized database on members and past giving
- the "prospect research" team he was putting together to evaluate potential supporters for the capital campaign
- the new slogan he was working on to prepare for the campaign: "Give Today—Grow Tomorrow"
- the brochures he and the staff were writing to support the campaign

Although everything on his list seemed pertinent, as Peter thought about it ahead of his meeting, he realized that he needed to focus on the upcoming campaign. But that depended on how the director reacted.

"Well, they're all important, aren't they?" the director said when Peter reviewed the list with him at their meeting. "Just try to squeeze them all in, don't you think?"

"Actually," Peter said, "I was thinking we could use this report to give the trustees a 'head's-up' on the campaign—sort of a warning shot, letting them know we're almost ready to launch it. Get them excited about it."

"Sounds right, Peter," the director said. "Put in what you think's important."

Peter was happy to get buy-in on his approach. He could write dozens of pages to cover all the topics he had listed and reviewed with the director, but the more he thought of it the more he believed the report presented an opportunity to push the campaign. That meant some of the points would have to be dropped or minimized. He wanted to concentrate on a single point, which he summarized for himself as he outlined his report: "After eight months of preparation, the Museum will launch its fundraising campaign under the slogan "Give Today—Grow Tomorrow."

Under that main point, he listed the subpoints that would support it: staff reorganization and new hires, the new database, and the prospect research effort. Then he would describe the new materials that were being prepared. Information about the annual appeal and the current membership program, although positive, were simply not relevant to the main point. So reluctantly he decided not to include them.

To make the evidence stronger, he decided to group the points in three segments:

- what's been done: reorganization, database
- what's under way: prospect research, preparation of brochures
- the schedule to accomplish the rest of the work and officially launch the campaign

To introduce the report, Peter decided to remind the trustees of the need for the campaign. Although they had tentatively approved going forward by creating Peter's position in the first place, he knew the trustees needed to be reminded of the necessity of the campaign, particularly given the relatively new concept of private fundraising.

He decided to start with a reminder of the active membership and annual appeal programs that had been in place for many years. That would give him a chance to note briefly where those efforts stood while at the same time helping the trustees to move from what they already knew to what he wanted to emphasize—that is, the importance of a capital campaign.

He drafted an introductory sentence: "Continued success in our annual appeal and membership program provides the best possible base for launching the major fundraising effort the museum requires to meet the challenges of future growth." After that, he decided, he would briefly report the current status of both programs. Then he would make his major point: "We're ready to launch the campaign." To support this point, he would review what had been done and what remained and then provide a schedule. He would conclude by reiterating the slogan—"Give Today—Grow Tomorrow."

Peter found that writing two pages was easy. He hoped the director would use the report exactly as he submitted it. He decided to make another appointment to review the draft in person.

Questions for Discussion

1. At least at the beginning of their discussion, who is more interested in the report—the director or Peter?
2. Should Peter have presented the list of topics at the first meeting with the director? Or asked the director to brainstorm topics with him?
3. Given the topics he came up with, is Peter's main point appropriate?
4. Has Peter organized his items in effective modules and aligned them in a convincing way?
5. Should Peter announce the slogan, "Give Today—Grow Tomorrow," in the opening or withhold it to create a dramatic ending? Which approach is more likely to gain the attention of Peter's various audiences?
6. Has Peter designed his report for easy access?
7. Does Peter's draft work as a component of another person's report? Does he need to find out more about other sections and tailor his work to those?

CHAPTER 6

Creating the Communication Product: Visuals and Text

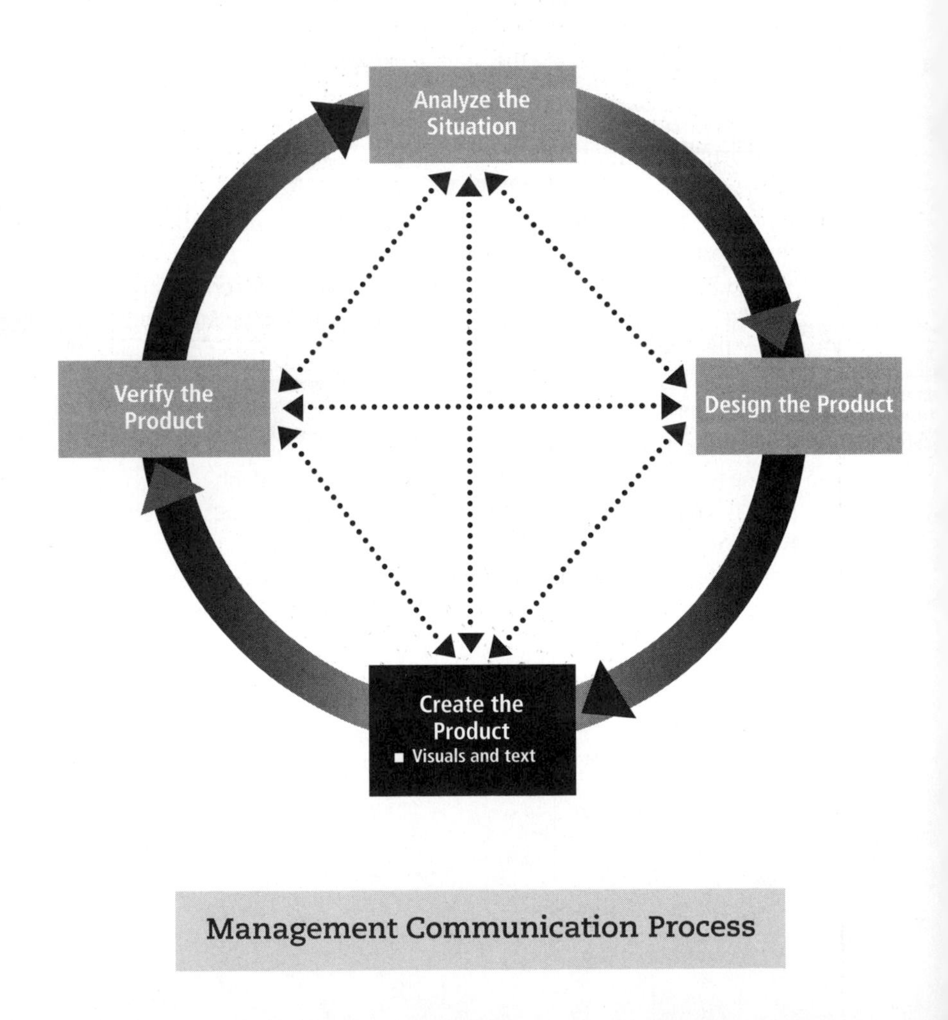

Management Communication Process

Good design takes you a long way toward a good communication product (see Chapter 5). This chapter offers guidelines for putting your outline in motion with the appropriate visuals and text and designing their appearance on a screen or a page.

Choosing Between Visuals and Text

As you assess the content of your message, decide what lends itself best to visual presentation and what's best in text (see Figure 6.1). In general, visuals are better at compressing a large amount of data and highlighting trends and comparisons. Text is better for developing an argument and controlling the meaning an audience derives from your information. Within that context, your choice reflects at least three factors: the nature of the information, the audience's visual/textual literacy and preferences, and the technological capacity of the media you are using.

Nature of the Information

First is the inherent nature of the information. Numerical information—for example, a budget or stock prices over time—fits well into a visual. Create a table to provide a close-up view of each item for analysis or a graph to show a broader picture over time, to trace a trend. If you need to explain those numbers—a flood in a factory, unexpected and wide currency fluctuations—you'll probably use text for that explanation.

Audience's Visual/Textual Literacy and Preferences

Second is the audience's visual and textual literacy and preferences. Can they read a balance sheet? Are they familiar with the conventions of a decision tree? Whatever their literacy, what do they prefer? Do they find textual explanations daunting? Boring? As a simple example, in giving directions from Point A to Point B, should you provide a map or a list of steps ("Take Route 48 for 3 miles to Lancaster Pike. Turn right . . .")? On some occasions, and especially with a mixed audience, consider using *both* visual and textual presentation. Just make sure that the visuals and the text don't contradict each other.

TYPE OF INFORMATION	VISUAL FORM
Physical space	Map, photograph, drawing
Dimensions of a 3-D object	Drawing, phantom view, table for measurements
Directions; point A to B	Map
Time: process	Flow chart with arrows
Time: continuous change in some variable (e.g., expenses, profit, market capitalization)	Line graph
Time: compare relationships among discrete items (e.g., video sales in the last five years)	Bar chart, table
Time: sequence of activities	Schedule (e.g., Gantt chart), flow chart
Parts of a whole (e.g., distribution of a retirement fund	Pie chart
Relationships among people	Organizational chart
Relationships among ideas	Diagram, decision tree
Budget	Table
Action plan (who does what, when, and status)	Table, Gantt chart
Demographic information interpreted for marketing purposes (e.g., what products sell where)	Map overlays
Cross-referencing between several variables (e.g., for each ski area in Utah: av. annual snowfall, Web address, base and top elevation, number of lifts, area of snow making . . .)	Matrix
Statistics	Table, computer-generated map

Figure 6.1 | Visuals That Do Business: Form Follows Information

Technological Capacity

Third is the technological capacity of the medium. Can you attach a photograph to your e-mail? Can your reader access that attachment? Is color appropriate in a document you're delivering on the Web—or will your audience print that document in black and white for further distribution and thus lose the message carried by color? Is a large-screen projection system available where you'll be giving your presentation? Adapt your use of visuals to the available technology (see Chapter 7).

Creating Visuals

In print, in presentations, and on the Web, you rely on visuals not only to convey information but also to draw attention and establish an atmosphere. Business audiences tend to be visually minded, so they understand and remember best what they see in pictures and numerical displays. Provide visuals to forecast an oral presentation for listeners, to help browsers navigate a Website (as in a site map), and to provide supporting evidence in any communication product. Choices include tables, graphs, diagrams and drawings, maps, photographs, and videos (see Figure 6.2).

Tables

Of the forms listed in Figure 6.1 and illustrated in Figure 6.2, a table is probably the least demanding to produce (once you have the data) and easiest to read. A table arranges words or numbers or both in rows (horizontal) and columns (vertical). Spreadsheets are a well known management example. Among other tasks, tables

- record numerical information consistently, as in a statistical presentation, budget, or price list.
- identify holes in your information where cells (intersections of rows and columns) are empty.
- document action plans.

Graphs

Another staple of business presentations and the business press is graphs (sometimes called *charts;* the terms tend to overlap). Where tables aid in close-up analysis of discrete items, graphs view information from

TABLES

- Label at the top
- Use a number (Table 1) or letter (Table A) for ease of reference
- Include units of measurement in the label, not after each item
- Make each table self-standing; provide explanatory information on the table itself, not in the surrounding text
- Use spacing to divide columns, not vertical lines

Table Title

Table A. Average Responses to Survey by Age Group
(scale: 5=important; 1=unimportant)

Column Heads

Item	18–22	23–27	28–32	33–42	43–47	Over 48

Action Plan

Table B. Proposed Task Plan

Task	Person Responsible	Target Completion Date
X	DCA	1/25
Y	BCD	1/20

Table emphasizing discrete items of information

Table 1. Average Monthly Closing Prices of Stock: Company A vs. Company B (in U.S. dollars)

Month	Company A	Company B
Jan	25.6	30.4
Feb	26.1	30.0
Mar	26.5	29.5
Apr	30.0	29.0
⋮	⋮	⋮
Sept	33.1	26.5
Oct	34.0	25.2
Nov	34.3	25.1
Dec	35.8	24.6

GRAPHS

Line Graphs

- Show a trend or continuous progression
- Limit each graph to 2 or 3 lines
- Use a series of graphs with parallel scales to show more lines
- Keep lines of equal width; a wider line may seem more important
- Label graphs outside the grid; be brief

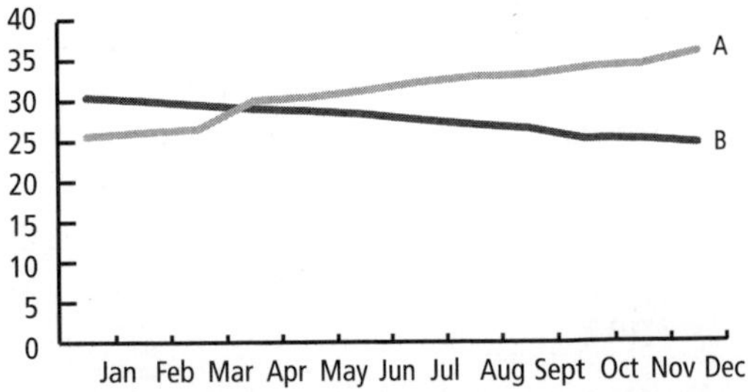

Figure 1. Average Monthly Closing Prices of Stock: Company A vs. Company B (in U.S. Dollars)

Figure 6.2 | Visuals That Do Business: Displaying Information

GRAPHS (cont.)

Bar Graphs
- Foster comparison of discrete items
- Stack bars horizontally for easy labeling
- Stack bars vertically to show change over time
- Avoid a 3-D look unless both the length and the volume of the bar are significant
- Arrange bars by length (short to long or long to short), alphabetically, or other

Segmented Bar Graphs
- Foster comparison of components of discrete items
- Use color or pattern to differentiate components

DIAGRAMS AND DRAWINGS

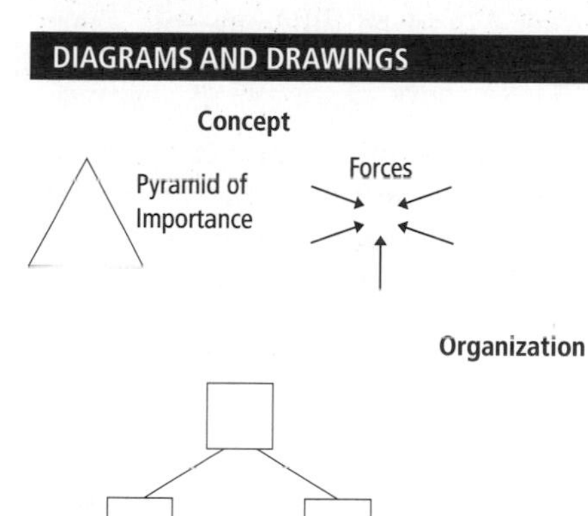

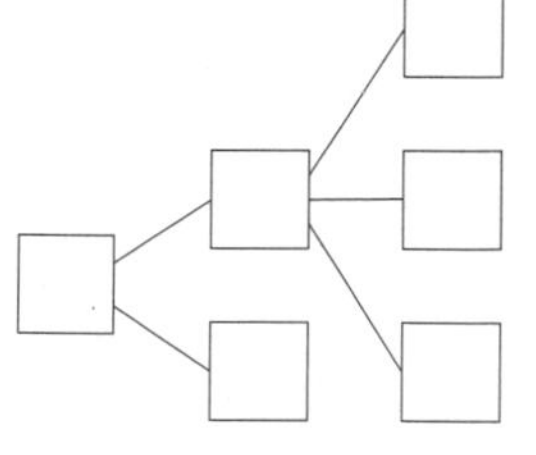

MAPS

- Indicate scale
- Zoom in as appropriate in parallel maps

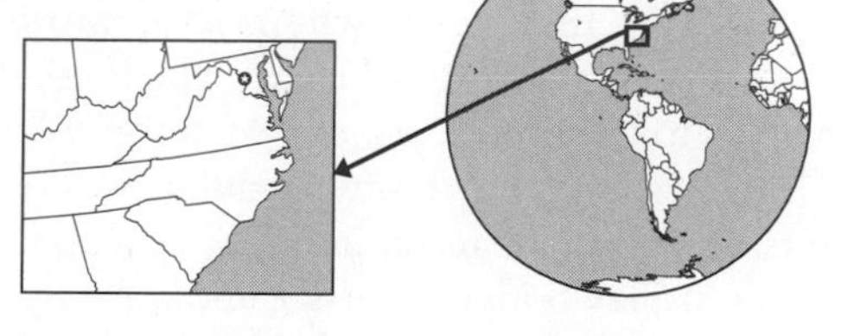

further out. A line graph, for example, shows trends and tendencies over time (profits, employment numbers, share prices, growth of the use of a software product, and the like). It's easy to see if things are going up or down—or up *and* down.

A bar graph fosters comparisons. A series of bars, for example, can show the transactions per minute of different software systems. In a more complex approach, you can segment the bars to display, for example, sources of income in four accounting firms. Each bar represents a firm, and the percentage contribution of each source (audit and accounting, tax advice, consulting, other) is represented by shading or other distinguishing marks in the bar. The same information might also appear in four pie charts, but the comparison would be less obvious, the charts would take up more room, and the tone would be different—pie charts are more likely used in communications aimed at general rather than professional audiences.

Although variations do exist, the conventions for creating tables and graphs are fairly well established, usually in software that creates them automatically from data you input. Most U.S.-produced line graphs, for example, place the units of measurement on the left vertical axis. But the British tend to place the units on the right.

Diagrams and Drawings

Whereas tables and graphs present discrete items and trends, especially in numerical data, diagrams and drawings help in *explaining* information and concepts. Such diagrams as organizational charts explain a structure, like the structure of a company, although the head may be at either the side or the top, with potential political implications. The format of an organizational chart can help writers arrange a brainstorming session into a coherent presentation (see Chapters 5 and 11). A flowchart is useful in explaining the steps in a process, including, for example, the tasks in a project (in a Critical Path Method diagram or a workplan). Be aware, however, that people who read from right to left may misunderstand the flow in a U.S.-based chart, which usually runs from left to right (use arrows to be sure, or arrange from top to bottom).

Drawings, which are often one-of-a-kind presentations, show, for example, the components of an object or a system (phantom or cut-away views that display both the outside and the parts inside) or a concept (like the Eating Right Pyramid on U.S. food products). Widely available clip art may be useful for a document or a presentation slide. But such art often lacks polish. Creating professional-looking drawings usually requires the assistance of a graphic artist working with a team of subject matter experts who test out various visual approaches (see Figure 6.2).

Maps

Traditional printed maps detail characteristics of the physical environment. Computer-displayed maps also allow interactivity: you can zoom in on details, make requests ("Show all courthouses"), or view the landscape or seascape in a head's-up orientation, from your point of view, not just the fixed point of view of someone flying overhead. A map framework can also accommodate other kinds of information; on a map of Europe, for example, you can overlay information about markets, energy use, types of industries, incidences of certain diseases, levels of education, and the like.

Photographs and Videos

Photographs help an audience understand the reality of a place, an object, an individual, or a group of people. Photographs are also dramatic and attractive and, with advances in scanning and digital cameras, increasingly easy to incorporate in e-mail, Websites, documents, and presentations. Similarly, videos can serve as excellent training tools, demonstrating, almost live, how to do something or how to behave in a particular circumstance. To reach wide audiences, videos can be streamed on computer screens across the Internet. Such an application, however, requires extensive memory and high-bandwidth connections. A photograph or video may also tell too much. Background items may distract the audience, and pictures of people may raise unintended readings. A photo of a training session that shows a man speaking while two women listen may be seen by some audiences as reinforcing gender stereotypes about leaders when the main purpose of the author was simply to show an active session.

Creating Text

Visuals are powerful devices for consolidating and conveying information and making a strong impression on an audience. To explain and interpret information, however, you'll often need to talk about it, either in person during an oral presentation or at a remove, in text on a page or on a screen. While creating such text is often a complex and messy activity, you can tame the process a bit if you think about just two forms: lists and paragraphs.

Lists

One form of text that appears both on the slides that accompany oral presentations and in documents is the list. Listing, with each element ideally no more than three or four lines, highlights discrete items of information and tells the audience that they should respond to each item separately, in turn. It also reinforces the equality of a series of items and helps the audience remember those items.

As you compose a list, keep in mind the principle of *parallelism* (see Chapter 5). Items must be parallel in both logic and expression. To be logically parallel, items in the list must be in the same category, for example:

- Advantages or disadvantages
- Causes of a current situation
- Effects of a cause
- Steps in a process
- Items in an inventory
- Names of clients
- Topics in an agenda

To be parallel in expression, all items must be stated in the same grammatical form. The first item sets the form that all others must follow—for example, in the list you've just read, all items are nouns or noun phrases.

List design aids skimming and focuses attention. In a document, place every item on a separate line, as in the list of categories above, to vary the look of text on the page or screen, increase white space and avoid dense blocks of text, reinforce the equality of each item, sort items for individual attention, and help the reader or listener remember. But enumerated lists take up more space, so use running text for lists (as in the last sentence) if you need to save space. Number the items to make it easy to refer to them in a discussion or to help the audience mark their place, as in performing the steps in a process. Use bullets or other icons if the sequence doesn't matter.

Paragraphs

A second form of text, and the major building block of documents, is the *paragraph*. A paragraph is composed of connected sentences (see Appendix A). Through paragraphing, you divide a total amount of content into modules that match the audience's ability to pay attention, assimilate information, and agree with your point. Consider the development, flow, and length of each paragraph within the context of other paragraphs.

Development First, to develop an effective paragraph, follow these linked strategies:

- Move from the general to the particular.
- Move from the familiar to the new.

Applying the first strategy means starting each paragraph, most of the time, with a topic sentence that announces the paragraph's point and forecasts, either implicitly or explicitly, the paragraph's approach:

> The housing market has saved the global economy from recession.

This topic sentence takes a stand—it makes a point—and implies an approach: the paragraph will offer an explanation to answer the reader's legitimate question, "How so?" Here's what follows:

> As stock prices, business investment, and profits have fallen and industrial production has slowed, average house prices in the United States, Europe, and elsewhere in the developed world have risen at a rate well ahead of inflation. Such high prices play a significant role in the economic cycle. Because housing is the single largest component of their wealth for most people in most countries, higher housing prices make them feel wealthier. Higher prices also allow homeowners to borrow more against that rising value. Thus they spend more, and that consumer spending offsets any downward pressure toward recession.

Note how repetition and transitional words (*also, thus*) help keep the explanation on track.

A topic sentence can also announce the approach explicitly:

> Here's a brief explanation of how the housing market has saved the global economy from recession.

Applying the second strategy means starting with a recap of information the reader knows (perhaps because you talked about it in the previous paragraph) and then moving to the new information you want to present to the reader:

> Given abundant signs of economic recovery [*presented as known information, probably from an earlier paragraph*], economists worldwide are revising their growth forecasts [new information, and the statement implies that the paragraph will provide examples]. The average prediction for GDP growth in the U.S. rose from 0.3 percent in December to 1.2 percent in April, according to a poll by McFadden Associates, a U.S. consulting firm. Other polls, too, indicate similar trends, with one, by Marks PLC, suggesting that growth over the year into the fourth quarter could rise to 3 or 4 percent.

Flow Second, paragraphs have to flow, that is, cohere internally and externally. To achieve flow within a paragraph, provide familiar information at the beginning of each sentence and new information at the end. Follow that advice doggedly, even mechanically, when you're having trouble getting your paragraph to cohere. It always works.

(earlier discussion on other tariffs)

> Recently, the U.S. Department of Commerce imposed a tariff of about 29 percent on Canadian softwood. Softwood is used to build houses, and about 30 percent of the softwood sold in the United States is imported from Canada. The Canadian government, some Americans charge, subsidizes its timber industry, selling wood at prices that do not reflect real production costs. Those prices are set by provincial governments, which have flexibility in determining how much they charge logging companies. Canadian logging companies, according to one U.S. authority, pay up to 60 percent less for standing trees than if they were forced to buy at a market-driven price.

To achieve external coherence—flow among paragraphs—make sure your basic structure is rational and sensible (see Chapter 5). In addition, reinforce that structure with linking statements in topic sentences ("Given abundant signs of economic recovery . . ."). To connect segments of a long document, consider including transitional paragraphs that help the reader look backward and forward:

> (looks backward)
> One-time start-up expenses and capital expenses thus account for the bulk of the costs associated with starting a small business. But entre-
> (announces a new topic)
> preneurs should also account for a third category: annual expenses, including salaries and wages, benefits, professional fees, rent and utilities, travel, supplies, and maintenance, all of which are discussed in this section.

Length Third, use paragraph length strategically. Don't fear short paragraphs (like the model you just read), especially in a setting of long ones. Long paragraphs are more common than they should be in management documents. In printed text, have at least one paragraph break on every page. Newspaper articles, aimed at quick reading, tend toward short paragraphs.

Designing the Screen or Page

To adapt a statement from *Alice's Adventures in Wonderland,* "Much of what you see depends on how *it* looks." In Chapter 5 you read about designing the deep structure of a communication product. This section provides guidelines for design at the surface level, for creating screens and pages that look good to the audience, a look that encourages reading, remembering, and complying and that reinforces your *brand,* that is, your particular style.

In addition to choosing between visual and textual form for expressing your content, consider the visual dimension of an entire communication product. New media and production methods help you meet the audience's expectation of good design. To solve complex design problems, you may need to work with a graphic artist. But in everyday practice, you can probably achieve the right look on your own if you pay attention to layout, typeface, and color. Figures 6.3 and 6.4 illustrate these strategies in the design of computer-generated presentation slides.

Layout

To lay out text and visuals on a page or screen, use three strategies: alignment, grouping, and headings.

Alignment In *aligning* text or visuals, you place them on an imaginary vertical or horizontal line. The most common vertical lines are the left and right margins. All text that begins at the left margin is read as equal in importance. In bulleted text and enumerated lists within paragraphs, indention along another vertical line subordinates those items:

All Things Considered
- One thing
- Another thing
    - A lesser part of that thing
    - Another lesser part of that thing
- A third thing

Aligning text between left and right margins horizontally is called *justification.* You have four choices: left justification (aligned at left), centered, right justification (aligned at right), full (aligned at both margins).

Left Centered Right Full

Unless you're working with a highly sophisticated word processing program, full justification may leave odd spaces between or within words. Most researchers advise that you use left justification for running text; the ragged right edge helps the reader's eye mark its place and odd spacing is avoided. Use other forms of justification only to highlight, as in a table of contents or a brief boxed example.

With the aid of a designer or using the layout function in presentation software, you can plan the *grid* of a screen or page, vertical and horizontal lines on which to place text and visuals. For a series of slides or documents, establish an appropriate grid and apply it to every item in the series. Such design parallelism reinforces the relationship among the items

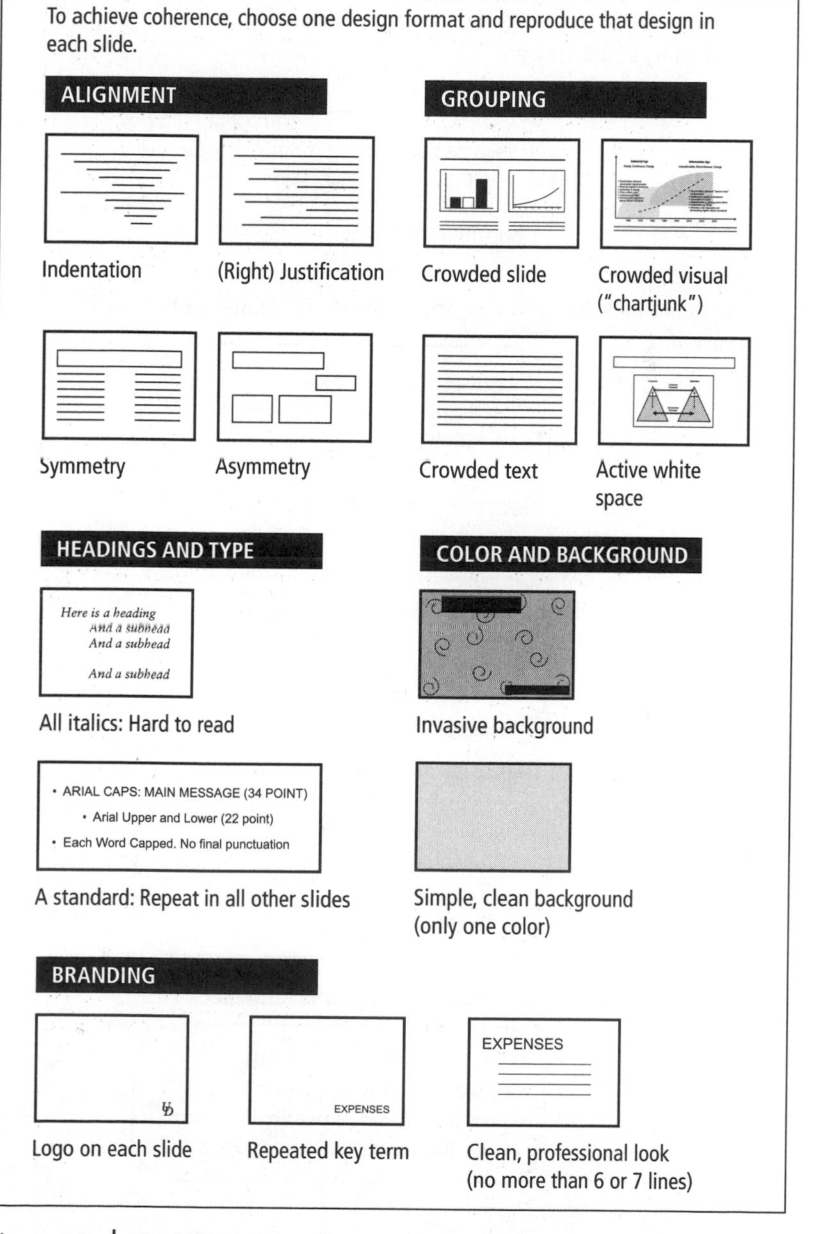

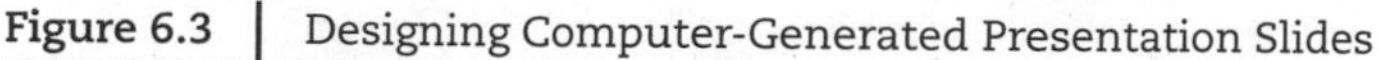
Figure 6.3 | Designing Computer-Generated Presentation Slides

Top-level title to market your message

- You can start a small business. . . . now
- Preparing a business plan

Key words to represent explicit sublevels

Expenses for Starting a Small Business
  One-time Start-up Expenses
  Capital Expenses
  Annual Expenses

Dimming or highlighting to help the audience navigate and to pace the presentation

Expenses for Starting a Small Business
  One-time Start-up Expenses
  Capital Expenses
  Annual Expenses

Nested sublevels. Use consistent wording (inconsistent: "Nonrecurring Start-up Costs").

One-time Start-up Expenses
  Legal
  Accounting
  Regulatory

Consistent design (This slide is inconsistent with the others in the series.)

One-time Start-up Expenses
  Legal and
  Accounting and
  Regulatory

No paragraphs. Think in terms of talking *points* not talk.

Words and Words and Words
and words and words and more
words and maybe a picture and more
words and words and words and words

Figure 6.4 | Creating Word Charts: Hierarchy and Parallelism

and ensures that they are considered as a whole. A current trend is for wide left margins on screens and slides. For printed text, such wide margins appear on left-hand pages, wide right margins on right-hand pages. On both screens and pages, the margin becomes the site for menus, headings, brief comments, small visuals, and the like.

Grouping Second, group similar elements to emphasize their similarity and to contrast them with differing elements. A paragraph, for example, is a grouping, its indention showing where a new point in a discussion begins. Windows on a screen group information that belongs together. As you group items in a draft arrangement, consider how they will appear to the reader in final form. For example, in a book layout and in bound manuals you can take advantage of a two-page spread. You have much less space on a screen or in an unbound report.

Use white space to divide the groups and provide emphasis for major content, separate visuals from text, and give the audience's eyes a rest. Strongly resist the temptation to fill the page or screen.

Headings Third, place headings strategically to signal the relationship among the groups. The more complex the text, the more you need headings. They are important in both access and design. Headings help readers skim for the gist of an argument, reinforcing and thus selling key points. Creating headings in your draft provides a check on the headings in your outline; change them if they no longer work or redo your text to conform to your earlier design.

Especially in persuasive documents and as the titles of slides in a persuasive presentation, prefer informative headings derived from your specific content to merely structural ones:

Informative	**Structural**
Expenses of Starting a New Business	Introduction
Implications of Economic Downturn	Discussion
Steps to Enhance Your Net Worth	Recommendations
Sales Increased 20% Over Last Year	Sales Figures

Following the logic of a hierarchy, avoid single subheads; when you divide something, you end up with at least two items. Readers also have an easier time if you create no more than three levels of heading in printed text and avoid having two headings abut. Place at least some introductory text under each heading. Finally, remember to keep all headings parallel in logic and expression (see Chapter 5).

Type

Headings provide quick access to the content of the message. They also offer an opportunity to apply another design tool: changes in type. In general, choose a different typeface for headings than you are using for running text, often a sans serif face (without hands and feet on the letters, like Arial) when the text is serif (like **Times Roman**). Differences in type size and font (**bold**, *italics*, shadowed, and the like) help to identify the level of a heading and thus of the text under the heading (Figure 6.5).

For running text, select a typeface that provides all the accents and special characters needed to express your message in the language of the communication product. Within the type you choose, you also can use uppercase or lowercase letters. In general, use a mix. Text in all capital letters draws attention but is slower to read because it forces readers to focus on one word at a time. It may also seem to shout:

THIS MESSAGE IS SENT TO REMIND YOU OF CURRENT CHOICES IN YOUR 401(k) PLAN.

Use all capital letters sparingly.

Changes in type size in running text identify text that is more im-

MAIN HEADING

The main heading (A-level heading) is centered, in all capital letters, boldface, Arial 14 points. Note the absence of serifs, extenders on the ends of the vertical and horizontal strokes of letters, as on the words you are reading in this running text, which is Times Roman.

B-level Heading

The B-level heading is left-justified, on its own line, in uppercase and lowercase letters, boldface, Arial 12 points.

C-level Heading. The C-level heading is indented, run in with the following paragraph, uppercase and lowercase letters, boldface, Arial 12 points.

Figure 6.5 | One Plan for Designating the Levels of Headings in a Print Document

portant (larger type) and less important (smaller type, as in footnotes and background information). Select the size to reflect the occasion and the audience.

10-point Times Roman

12-point Times Roman

24-point Times Roman

For documents, 12 point is usually appropriate, although you may use a larger size for text addressing children and the elderly. For slides, you may want to place main headings in 35–40 point and lists under those heads in 20–24, using a larger type size when the text will be displayed in a large room. Changes in font also help to emphasize, as in words and passages in italics or boldface. Just be careful not to overuse these options and, in particular, not to display an entire segment or product in italics, which is hard to read.

Color

If the technology for delivering your communication product allows, use color in addition to type to clue the reader about how to read and to establish a desired atmosphere. It's rare to find a colorless Website, for example. Color photographs on a homepage draw attention. Color also helps an audience navigate a site: a change in the color in linking words or phrases, for example, reminds readers about which links they have followed.

In printed text, screening a word, line, or paragraph in color highlights the message presented. Yellow is a favorite for this task, a reminder, perhaps, of how students use yellow highlighters to mark up their textbooks. In addition, a consistent color screen can identify certain types of information throughout a document or presentation: all quotations, perhaps, in green; examples or asides in blue. Color tabs or edge strips help readers zero in on a section of a report they're interested in. Color can also identify heading levels—all main heads in red, for example.

In choosing colors for a screen presentation, keep in mind the messages color sends. Those messages vary across cultures; red, for example, is associated with danger in North America but with joy and festivity in China. Americans wear black at a funeral, indicating mourning, and white at a wedding, meaning hope; people in India wear white at a funeral, symbolizing purity and the eternal soul. One researcher has found different interpretations of color among different professional group (G. E. Jones, *How to Lie with Charts,* San Francisco: Sybek, 1995, 205):

Color	Financial Managers	Healthcare Professionals	Control Engineers
Blue	Corporate, reliable	Dead	Cold, water
Green	Profitable	Infected, bilious	Nominal, safe
Red	Unprofitable	Healthy	Danger

Keep in mind, too, the difficulty of seeing white text on a light background, for example, or red text on black or blue. If your audience will need to print out your screens or slides, consider using black text on white background, which prints easily.

Branding

Good design in itself may please the audience, but more important is its service to your message—and to you. The design helps the reader quickly access the information needed, understand that information, and comply with any request or proposal your message conveys. It makes reading comfortable. The good design of presentation slides similarly reinforces your oral remarks and fosters comprehension and action. Avoid being seduced by readily available templates with names like "Dad's tie" and "artsy." Your audience may be all too familiar with these and discount your presentation if it relies blindly on them. Instead, create your own template for a professional presentation (see Figure 6.3).

In addition, good design builds and heightens credibility. Like the other products you and your organization create, your communication products reflect a distinctive *brand.* The design of screens and pages promotes that brand by reinforcing your professionalism and strengthening the trust between you and your audience, the customers of your message.

SCENARIO

Preparing Texts and Visuals for a Presentation

After three years as assistant, Jorge Manzilla was appointed director of employee relations by John Cole, who became vice president for administration at Central Medical Center (CMC), a large city hospital in Los Angeles. Jorge was eager to implement changes in the human resources (HR) function. Although Jorge believed that John had been well meaning and effective, he also knew that John was more interested in financial management and therefore well suited for his new position. While he still reported to John, Jorge was now in charge of HR and eager to adopt new techniques, beginning with an expanded orientation program for new employees.

Jorge and John met with Dorothy LePage, M.D., CMC's chief operating officer, to discuss the orientation program. "John and I are happy you're taking this on, Jorge," Dorothy said at the beginning of the meeting. "Our employees are the heart of CMC, and with our high turnover and the problems recruiting health care professionals, we really have to orient new hires well."

"Not my strongest skill," John added with a laugh. "I realize that, and I know you have good ideas, Jorge, and like Dorothy I'm glad you're in charge. What do you have in mind?"

Jorge described his plan to expand the orientation to a full day and listed the topics he hoped to cover. "I thought Dorothy should be the first speaker, to welcome people and discuss our history and mission statement. Then, John, I hope you'll give an overview of the organizational structure and say something about our financial situation."

"The org chart's in the handbook," John said, "and as for finances, why would they be interested in that?"

"John," Dorothy interjected, "Jorge's running this now, and I like his idea. You can't just tell people where the organizational chart is in the handbook. You have to walk people through it. And we want people to know about finances so they can be a part of the team."

John laughed. "You're right, Dorothy. Now I can see how smart I was to hire Jorge in the first place and to promote him. What else do you have in mind, Jorge?"

"After you and Dorothy do the big picture," Jorge replied, "I was going to focus in on the HR process, give a sort of overview of how it works, from hiring through promotion, termination, salary increases, and so on. Then I'd like to highlight some special topics: a review of benefits, employee discipline, training, the sexual harassment policy, and then end up with sessions on customer relations."

"I love it, Jorge," Dorothy said. "Especially the customer relations training. We really need that."

"What will the docs think?" John asked. "They don't like ideas like 'customer relations.'"

"Nurses, either," Dorothy added.

"I thought we'd break out the groups on that one," Jorge said. "One of the problems with the orientation is that it includes every new employee, from custodian to M.D. For some of the topics, that's okay because everyone is treated the same. But on customer relations particularly, I thought we could split into groups—one for support staff, one for professionals."

"Which sort of reinforces the divisions, doesn't it?" Dorothy asked. "But I see your point. Maybe you can think about it a bit more. And speaking of divisions, how are you going to handle the language one?" Between one-third and one-half of CMC's employees were native speakers of Spanish.

When he had been head of employee relations, John had resisted Jorge's recommendation to provide a Spanish version of the employee handbook, although he had supported Jorge's use of visuals for conveying instructions to lower-skilled staff with limited English.

"Still want to do a Spanish version of the handbook?" John asked. When Jorge said he did, John surprised him by agreeing. "And I can see that your visuals really work. Why don't you use lots of them in the presentation, so everyone can follow?"

"But again, is that going to just reinforce divisions?" Dorothy asked.

"Maybe not so much reinforce them as help us overcome them," Jorge said. "If we do it right. So shall I prepare more materials, visual and textual, and in both languages, so you two can review all this before we schedule the orientation?"

Dorothy and John agreed, and they set an appointment in five days to review Jorge's drafts.

Questions for Discussion

1. For which of the "special topics" would you advise Jorge to divide the new employees into groups? What groupings would you suggest—for example, random (merely to produce appropriately sized groups), by organization level (professional, staff, etc.), by language, by organizational divisions (medical, clerical, administrative, etc.)? Why?
2. For each topic, what kind of visuals (tables and graphs, drawings, photos and videos, etc.) would you suggest? Why—what advantages and disadvantages does each type have?
3. What surface design techniques (layout, type, color) should Jorge employ for the various topics? Why?

4. Should Jorge use both visuals and texts for all or some parts of the presentations? What advantages and disadvantages does this approach offer over using merely one type of presentation? What material is best conveyed visually? What is best conveyed textually?
5. How do you think Jorge Manzilla and John Cole are handling the political aspects of their interactions, considering that John formally held Jorge's position and remains his manager?
6. Is Jorge getting buy-in from the two executives for his approach? How would you advise him to do so as he moves to the next phase of his work—preparing drafts of materials?

CHAPTER

7 Creating the Communication Product: Emphasis on Speaking

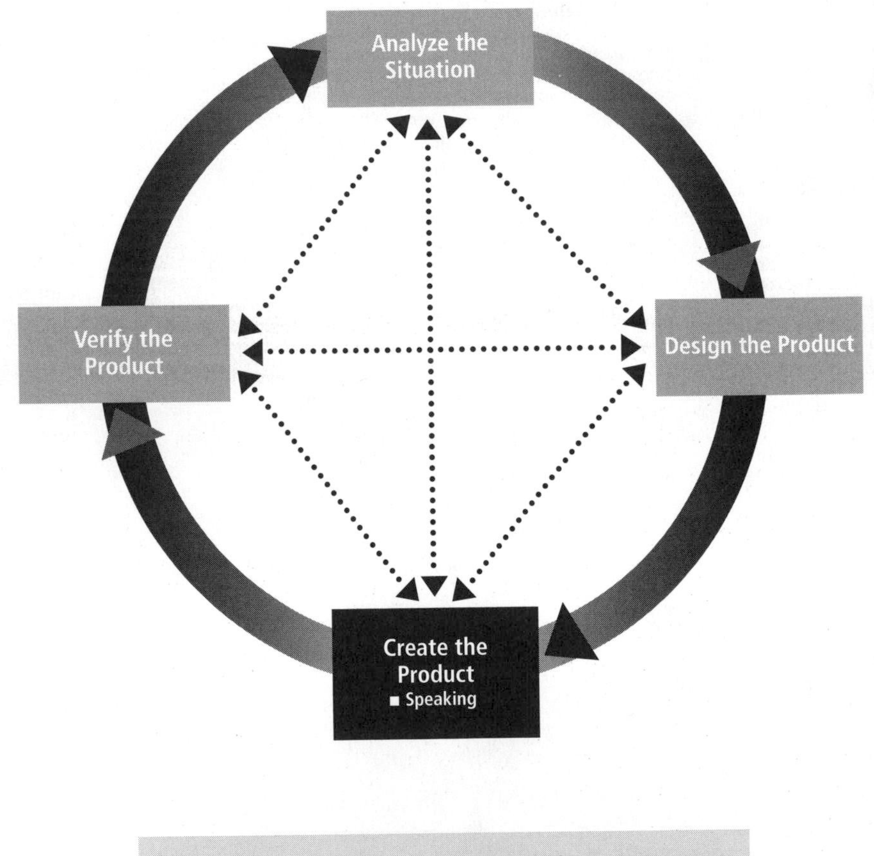

Management Communication Process

Speaking and writing have much in common, especially given electronic presentation software that provides text to back up a talk and e-mail that often reproduces conversation in text. Thus similar design strategies apply to both even if the communication products are different (see Chapters 5 and 6). This chapter shows those strategies at work in managerial situations that foreground speaking: interpersonal communication, meetings, and oral presentations. Chapter 8 looks at some common situations that foreground writing: memos, letters, e-mail, proposals, and reports. All these speaking and writing situations are often tightly defined; you find yourself working within the box of conventions for that genre or occasion (see Chapter 5). Start with those conventions as you prepare a communication product. But to establish a personal brand, you may need to engage in some outside-the-box communication strategies.

Interpersonal Communication

Talking and listening effectively with another person or in small groups are critical components of your role as a manager. Such conversations require what one researcher calls "with-it-ness," an ability to ask appropriate questions, take turns and accommodate rapidly to what others say, and use and respond to nonverbal signals.

Asking Appropriate Questions

Conversations build momentum through questions and answers. To show your interest, ask questions that invite more than a yes or no answer ("What factors in the economic or cultural setting of Vancouver do you think favor our expansion there?" *rather than* "Do you think Vancouver will work?"). Watch for perhaps unintended negative slants to your questions ("Anyone familiar with this situation would agree with our decision, don't you think?" or "Do you have anything at all to say about this?").

Taking Turns

Talking also becomes true conversation, rather than monologue, through turn taking. Recognize when it is time for you to talk and when you should stop talking. Don't interrupt, or talk over the end of someone else's comment, or complete the other's sentences. Allow for some silence in which everyone can regroup.

Accommodate to what others say (see Chapter 10 for more about listening skills). You devalue another person's ideas or story if, after he or she has spoken, you simply launch into your own story or ideas. You can also cause ill will if you let yourself be distracted and don't keep up with what someone is saying, or if you decide before others have stopped speaking that what they are saying isn't worth listening to or is wrong. Instead, hold judgment, extract the speaker's main point and evidence, and then let that information be a platform for your next remarks:

Speaker One: . . . for all these reasons, Montreal seems like the right place to start our expansion in Canada.
Speaker Two: So let's put Montreal on the list. I'd also like to consider Vancouver since it has . . .

Using Nonverbal Signals

Because words convey only part of the message, pay attention to the nonverbal signals that may reinforce, amplify, or contradict the words (see Figure 7.1). These vary across cultures, which means that you have to watch carefully what people do as well as what they say when you engage in cross-cultural exchanges and perhaps ask for advice to make sure you are sending and receiving the right signals. At least in Western culture, when you engage in a conversation or give a talk,

- look the other in the eye.
- maintain a welcoming posture (crossing your arms over your chest, for example, seems unwelcoming).
- sit or stand at a comfortable distance from the other—and read their body language (are they moving away? moving toward you?) to determine that distance.

Be aware, too, of messages in the setting. When you sit behind a desk, that barrier may reinforce your power over the other person; but if you aim for good rapport, come out from behind the desk. Pay attention to cosmetics and costuming. Someone who finds your perfume offensive may thus discount your credibility. If you dress formally for an important visitor, who honors you, too, by dressing formally, then that common dress may enhance the conversation. If someone speaks too loudly (*vocalics*) or has an accent that's hard to understand or seems to indicate a lack of education, those signals may undercut the importance or validity of a message or of the individual speaking. Avoid signs, like looking at your watch

CATEGORY	EXAMPLES
Organismics	Physical characteristics (attractiveness, height, weight, physique)
Cosmetics	Chemical enhancements, applied cosmetic applications, and cosmetic surgical interventions
Costuming	Clothing and clothing accessories
Haptics	Effects of touch
Kinesics	Effects of body movements and body postures
Oculesics	Effects of eyes
Vocalics	Effects of voice
Chronemics	Effects of time
Proxemics	Effects of space, spatial relationships
Objectics	Effects of objects wittingly or unwittingly placed in the environment

Figure 7.1 Categories of Nonverbal Communication
Source: Courtesy of Donald B. Egolf, Ph.D., University of Pittsburgh.

or staring out a window, that indicate boredom. In important conversations, especially between you and a superior, consider taking notes. You'll not only be able to recall main points better later on, but the note taking itself signals your seriousness about the interview.

Conducting Conversations Across Cultures

In general, consider these elements of interpersonal communication style, especially as you conduct conversations across cultures:

- *Show of emotion.* Would the other person expect you to show emotion? Is reserve (the British "stiff upper lip") more appropriate?
- *Self-disclosure.* How clear is the distinction between public and private information? Should you reveal private information only to close friends? Will the other person *expect* you to ask about family and other private issues?
- *Directness.* Should requests be phrased directly ("Attend the meeting on 3 May") or indirectly ("It would be terrific if you could join us at the meeting on 3 May," "Will you please join us on 3 May?")?
- *Imposition.* How comfortable are you—and is the other person—with your asking a favor? Is self-reliance more valued? Is asking a favor taken as losing face?
- *Interaction with strangers.* Is ease in such interaction valued in your culture (as in the U.S.)? Should you engage strangers in conversation on a train or a plane?
- *Names and titles.* Will the other person expect you to use his name with some frequency in the conversation ("As you suggest, William, this approach has a few disadvantages."), a typically effective strategy in a U.S. context? Or will the other person find that annoying?
- *Leave taking.* How extensive should your expression of goodbye be after a conversation or a meeting? Is merely exiting the room enough? Or is that rude? Should you make a specific statement about the meeting or event ("I think we accomplished a lot today, thanks to your good insights. Thanks so much.")?

Meetings

Interpersonal skills are called on, too, in a meeting—an informal or formal gathering of various numbers of individuals. Through your participation in meetings you advance organizational and personal goals, engender trust, and demonstrate technical and interpersonal competence.

Face-to-face meetings heighten the intensity of attention paid to the core issue under discussion (for advice about *virtual* meetings, see Chapter 11). They have a greater emotional charge and greater potential for creative thinking than, for example, a series of e-mails circulated to the same people. That charge comes from the *interactivity* of a meeting. Performing well at a meeting requires

- a willingness to hear evidence, to compromise, perhaps to change your mind when the evidence presented is convincing.
- enough self-confidence to speak out in the group and to let others speak out.
- civility, that is, polite behavior that respects the opinions and points of view of others.

While they can be powerful management tools, meetings are also expensive, in participants' time and travel costs, so resist any tendency to see a meeting as the default option in problem solving. Instead, reserve meetings for situations when such a gathering is the only means to get the job done. In those situations, prepare well, lead or participate well, and follow through.

Preparing

First, make sure a meeting is the right approach to achieving your communication goal. Face-to-face meetings work well for

- brainstorming (see Chapter 5).
- building trust, for example, in a team that will later work mainly via computer.
- monitoring progress on a project, particularly one with problems.
- gaining buy-in for a concept or new procedure.
- building consensus on a controversial issue.
- coming to a decision.

Then if you are the manager responsible for the meeting select the attendees, determine and announce the meeting logistics, and write the agenda.

Attendees For routine meetings of project teams, standing committees, and the like, the list of attendees generally mirrors membership on the team or committee. Under some circumstances, a visitor may be called in to provide special expertise on an issue, or some members may be excused if their own area of interest will not be discussed.

Special-purpose meetings pose more questions about who should attend. The leader needs to balance political concerns, like inclusiveness, with functional ones, like making sure the meeting doesn't bog down in disagreements or in the logistics of finding a common meeting time among too many attendees. Make sure the group represents the expertise needed to get the job done and attitudes needed to work together toward that outcome.

Logistics As with all communication products, the setting and timing of a meeting are critical. For example, sitting around a conference table encourages interaction among all attendees (an all-channel communication network); sitting in rows that face a leader encourages questions and answers between the audience and the leader but less interaction within the audience (wheel communication network). Timing, too, matters, in several senses. Give timely notice of the meeting, preferably a week or two advance notice so attendees can adjust their calendars. If you ask attendees to select the best meeting time from several options, respond as soon as possible with a message confirming a specific time. In your announcement concerning the time and place for a meeting, make sure you give both starting and ending times and hold to that limit. An hour is probably enough for most routine meetings. If you think you'll need more than that amount of time, schedule two or more short meetings. If you schedule a meeting early or late in the day, keep in mind that some people may have difficulties adjusting their commuting routine or child-care arrangements to accommodate those times.

Agenda The phrase "seize the agenda" suggests the power of this meeting tool as an aid in exercising both organizational and personal control. An agenda

- confirms the goals and approach of the meeting.
- shapes attendee expectations.
- provides a structure that controls participant interaction.
- builds momentum toward a decision or resolution.
- structures the documentation of the meeting's accomplishments.

Figure 7.2 provides advice on creating an agenda to foster meeting productivity. Circulate the agenda before the meeting, probably in an e-mail message. Limit the number of agenda items (consider seven the outside limit) to avoid overwhelming attendees. You may need to categorize items and display only the major categories in the published agenda; you can add subcategories in the meeting itself. If your first agenda item is "announcements," a typical opener, reconsider: it may be best to attach a statement of those announcements in the e-mail so that you can move directly into discussion items once the meeting begins. The amount of detail

Logistics

- Confirm the date, time, place, and duration of the meeting.

Purpose

- State briefly but specifically, with a focus on both process and outcome.

  Example: After a brief presentation by Jules and Jim about the proposed expansion into Canada (please read the attached proposal before the meeting), we'll encourage general discussion of its merits and try to come to a consensus on whether to proceed.

Items for Discussion

- Arrange strategically.

  Example: Old business before new business (the familiar before the new), topics that you anticipate will engender only brief discussion before those that need more extensive treatment, non-controversial items before controversial ones. If you think attendees won't pay attention until the controversy comes up, however, start with that.

Role Assignments

- If appropriate, note which individuals are responsible for particular items.

  Example:

  (Peter) Competitor Analysis: Starbucks
  (Steve) Competitor Analysis: Café Deux

Attachments

- Attach to an e-mail notice any documents that may be needed as background for discussion.

  Examples:

  Standing reports (like those of the secretary or treasurer of an organization)
  Announcements (to save time that might otherwise be spent reading them in the meeting)
  Special reports central to the meeting's purpose.

Figure 7.2 | Components of an Agenda

given in the agenda and the rigidity of the approach (for example, whether time limits are designated for each item) reflect an organization's protocols and a leader's personal style.

Unless the agenda is long or requires a particular format, paste it into the message (rather than as an attachment) for ease of reading at once. Add a brief explanation at the start of the e-mail for anyone needing a special head's-up about the meeting—for example, acknowledging someone who has a more-than-ordinary interest in the meeting's outcome, perhaps to encourage him or her to speak up or to temper comments; or devoting special attention to someone of higher rank than the rest of the meeting's attendees. While you have a right to expect attendees to bring a copy of the agenda with them to the meeting, some may not, so it's wise to have copies available or to display the agenda on a screen or white board in the meeting room.

Leading a Meeting

If you are leading the meeting, appoint attendees to any roles necessary to achieve the meeting's goals and let them know their role before the meeting. One person (not the leader) should take notes. If the discussion may be subject to controversy or misunderstanding, consider appointing another person to review those notes and write up the minutes. If attendees will be asked to vote on company policies or actions, appoint someone who knows organizational protocols to oversee the voting and another person to count the votes. For large meetings that address major issues, consider engaging the services of a meeting facilitator. In promoting and overseeing the interaction of participants, the facilitator frees you to take a more actively engaged role in the substance of the discussion. The facilitator may also incorporate strategies of electronic meeting systems to achieve consensus, including surveys of all participants and polling (see Chapter 11). But when you are in charge, manage both the discussion and the participants as the following sections suggest.

Managing the Discussion Begin the discussion on time and with a statement of the meeting's purpose and duration. Note any constraints and procedures that apply to the discussion or develop special procedures if necessary. For example, you might remind attendees that they should not reveal to anyone else the content of the discussion (if that's a constraint); agree on a time limit for all comments (no one can speak for more than two minutes at a time); agree on a method for taking turns in discussion (everyone should jump in as the occasion warrants or speakers should wait to be recognized by the leader). Note up front any changes in the agenda (like a new or a deleted item or a change in the order of items). Otherwise, move through the agenda as announced, respecting any time limits imposed. If attendees suggest items to consider that are not on the agenda, record them and offer to discuss them at a future meeting. End the meeting at the time set in your meeting announcement, or extend that time only after you've gathered a consensus of participants for such an extension. Schedule any future meetings.

Managing the Participants Even more important, and more difficult, than keeping your eye on the clock and the agenda is encouraging the give-and-take that is a meeting's main advantage over other forms of communication. Move as quickly as possible from your opening remarks to the discussion; the longer you let attendees remain passive the harder it may be to encourage active participation. Take your own notes on the meeting's progress—not necessarily for the minutes but as reminders to you of who said what and thus who needs to be heard from further.

To rein in those who are talking too much, use a direct, polite statement ("Sam, that's terrific, but perhaps we should hear from others about this."). To encourage participation from those who have been quiet or whose body language indicates discontent or boredom, ask a question based on the kind of contribution they might make ("Gene, you've been involved with other expansion projects. What do you think of this?"). If momentum is dragging, enter the discussion to clarify points that seem to be diffuse, present a new way to look at an item, or pose a question to everyone. Before ending the meeting, make sure everyone agrees on the meeting's outcome, even if that outcome is a summary statement outlining the terms of a disagreement.

Participating in a Meeting

As an attendee, perform any role you've agreed to. In addition, *participate.* In a formal meeting, wait to be recognized before you speak, remembering your point (maybe by jotting down a note or two on the agenda) even when two or three others may speak before you. And listen to those speakers; if your point has already been covered before it's your turn, acknowledge that and simply state agreement with the earlier point.

Pay attention to turns in the discussion. It's easy to let a new topic slip by while you craft your own statement about an earlier issue; when you come to speak, you're off the topic. Keep up to speed. Don't fall in love with your own voice, and read the signals, like frowns or the shuffling of paper, when others feel you have been speaking too much. Stop, maybe even by explicitly recognizing your dominance of the conversation ("Oops, sorry, I think I've been talking too much."). Such an overt statement may help you regain favor from the other attendees.

Because it provides a common means of communication among

people who speak different languages, most of whom have probably studied it, English often serves as the international language of business meetings. The presence of even one American in a meeting with, say, German counterparts may send the meeting into English if that American does not speak German. Participants forced into English, however, may resent the need to make that adjustment and continue side conversations in their native language. In addition, recognize that there are several Englishes, including variants in the United States, the U.K., Singapore, and India. Exercise patience to overcome the tendency for differences in accents and dialects to frustrate the meeting process (see Figure 7.3).

Following Through

After the meeting, circulate the minutes, probably in an e-mail, to all attendees as well as to others who may be affected by the meeting's outcome. Align the minutes to the agenda; indicate the major points covered

Speaking and Listening Across Languages

- Be especially patient: discussions where language itself becomes an issue tend to take longer and be more tiring.
- In small groups and meetings, avoid side conversations in another language because these may reduce group trust and engender suspicion.
- Focus on content: don't correct a speaker's pronunciation or grammar.
- Don't rush in to supply what you think is a word or phrase eluding the speaker.
- Speak carefully but avoid the loud and monotone delivery some U.S. managers consider the essence of communicating across cultures ("THE RECOVERY PLAN REQUIRES 5 STEPS")
- Ask for clarification, politely, if you can't understand what someone has said.
- Streamline your vocabulary and use formal English, avoiding slang.
- Avoid jokes and diversions.
- If an interpreter is aiding the interaction, talk with the other participants, not the interpreter.

Figure 7.3 | Speaking and Listening Across Languages

in the discussion of each item, any decisions made, any future actions to be taken (and by whom), and the next decision point or meeting.

Presentations

Even if you'd prefer to do almost anything else, you are certain to give oral presentations during your managerial career. To do so, you may sit at a conference table, stand alone at a podium, or sit or stand with others on a project team. You may address any number of people from a few to hundreds. The audience may consist of people inside or outside your organization: managers reviewing a project report; clients listening to a sales presentation; sponsors assessing a potential research project; representatives of the media questioning your organization's behavior, policies, or potential. This chapter focuses on face-to-face presentations, but you are likely to give virtual presentations, too, in your career (see Chapter 11).

Talking Face to Face

Face-to-face presentations are a staple of management. One important reason is the heightened emotional charge that comes when a presenter and an audience are actually together in the same room. That charge can lead to creativity, understanding, and action that might not occur in any other way. Another reason is the opportunity for direct interactivity, with all the cues of body language as well as words and visuals, when important decisions are on the line. Before your company hires a financial adviser, or accepts the new business process system recommended by a team of consultants, you'll want to size them up in person to obtain the most realistic reading you can about who they are and whether you can trust them. If your organization is in trouble or otherwise on a public agenda, then someone, preferably the CEO, will address the print and broadcast media to build trust and maintain the company's brand (see Appendix C). Presentations, too, often precede decisions on hiring and promotions within a company, for similar reasons. Can the candidates think on their feet? Do they have a commanding *presence*? Such elements of a personal brand play a significant role in hiring and promotion decisions.

Choosing an Approach

In developing your talk, analyze the situation in terms of the communication model, especially the culture of the setting, your goal, the audience, and your relationship with that audience (see Chapters 3 and 4). Then select an approach to match that analysis. Three are common: impromptu, outlined, and scripted.

Impromptu An impromptu talk is given on the spur of the moment and is often highly interactive. The approach invites informality and is particularly suited to small groups. During a meeting, you may be asked to comment, even at some length, about your area of expertise as it illuminates an issue under discussion. The convener of the meeting may provide fair warning about that request in advance. Your expertise is clear; you don't need further research to present a convincing argument. An impromptu talk allows you to direct material well to the audience because you're composing on the spot, letting their questions or interest expressed in earlier discussion shape what you say. Some people, however, given this occasion, tend to digress, talk too long, and lack focus. If you are uncomfortable at composing a presentation on the spot, try to avoid this approach.

Outlined Instead, if you have a choice, make an outline (see Chapter 5). Let a smart reading of an agenda alert you to the possibility that you may be called on for a presentation. Prepare even when you know you may not have to speak. In your outline and notes, focus on the main point and assemble significant supporting evidence. Align your approach to units of time in the same way that journalists align their stories to the requirements of space. Start with the most important points first, then lead into more detail as time allows.

For any simple, impromptu-like presentation, within a meeting or as a stand-alone exercise, write your outline and notes on a lined pad or on separate note cards, one for each major point. For more complex and lengthy presentations bring in the appropriate technology to help you share your outline with the audience (Figure 7.4).

Scripted At the other extreme from making impromptu remarks is using a script. A scripted presentation takes a formal approach and is especially suited to large groups. It does not invite interaction, except perhaps in a question-and-answer period at the end. It aims at ultimate control. Although scriptwriters (often not the final presenter) may evoke a casual tone, the remarks usually sound like the printed text they actually are. Writers craft the remarks in anticipation that the script will be reproduced *as* text, in a newspaper or on the Web. Often, they write in the shadow of an attorney or two whose counsel has been sought to ensure wording on the right side of a controversial or difficult issue.

When you write or approve the script of a talk, keep in mind the differences between how people listen and how they read. Texts to be heard have to be less dense and less complex than texts to be read, even if the audience will be given the prepared text in advance. Remember the long history of reading aloud as a strategy for helping children to go to sleep. Many audiences revert to childlike, passive behavior when a speaker starts reading a talk. To keep the audience listening actively, use short sentences that provide frequent breaks. In addition, avoid elaborate phrasing that is hard for an audience to unpack and then process. Avoid, too, an odd series of sounds ("silvicultural practices surfacing in serious discussions of long-leaf, slash-pine forests") that can trip you up as a speaker.

Choosing the Appropriate Technology

Choose the appropriate technology to support your approach (Figure 7.4). The technology helps you to capture information as you and the audience communicate and to display materials you prepared in advance. When you make information visible, you aid the audience in navigating a presentation and you document main points and supporting evidence. You may sketch ideas on a napkin in an informal conversation or use a flip chart or a white- or blackboard in a small group. With larger groups, and for an outlined or scripted presentation, consider taking advantage of electronic presentation software (see Chapter 6).

Good use of technology often helps to sell the message, enhance the speaker's credibility, and make even a mediocre performer seem dynamic. You may devote most of your preparation time to developing slides, arranging a live Internet connection, or pulling together video clips. Just make sure the technology is a feature of the environment for the presentation and that you are comfortable working with it. Make sure, too, that the audience expects and welcomes it. Elaborate technology may reduce the effectiveness of your message with an audience whose culture is more low-key.

TECHNOLOGY	ADVANTAGES	DISADVANTAGES
Blackboard or whiteboard	Widely available Fosters discussion and writing on the spot Paced to the audience's ability to assimilate	Presenter has to turn back on audience Hard to read if handwriting is poor Undramatic Accommodates only sketches, not finished visuals No permanent record
Flip chart	Low technical demands Movable Interactive Paced to audience's ability to assimilate Provides a removable record Can be prepared in advance	Hard to read if handwriting is poor Undramatic Limited to small group for good viewing Accommodates only sketches, not finished visuals
Transparency (overhead)	Easy to prepare in advance Easy to arrange and rearrange Easy to write on during discussion Visible in a lighted room Displayed while presenter faces room Accommodates finished visuals	Requires an overhead projector May seem outdated May be hard to see whole screen

Figure 7.4 Common Technology for Displaying Visuals in a Presentation

TECHNOLOGY	ADVANTAGES	DISADVANTAGES
35-mm slides	High resolution for photographs Good visibility in large room	Have to go through each in order Requires a darkened room
Large-screen computer display	Accommodates multiple media: video, audio, animation, sophisticated visuals Can display content from the Internet Dramatic, sometimes dazzling	Requires laptop and projection system More subject to technical failures May seem intimidating, not welcoming of discussion Can't be changed during the presentation Room may need to be darkened

Figure 7.4 Cont. | Common Technology for Displaying Visuals in a Presentation

Designing the Presentation

Whatever your approach and the technology you choose, your presentation has to fit within the box of *time*. In addition, at least in a Euro-American context, it has to fit within the box of conventions concerning how a talk usually begins, proceeds, and ends (Figure 7.5). Within each segment, local conditions for your talk may dictate a specific design—for example, always opening a sales presentation by acknowledging the top salesperson of the period.

Length You may choose the length of your talk or, more likely, that length will be set for you: a 20-minute presentation among others in an orientation session, a one-hour segment in a consultant's overview before going live with the implementation of a new system, a 15-minute candidate's briefing to a hiring committee. Obviously, and most important, confirm the allotted time in advance and respect that limit.

Introduction
Time ______________
- Preview. ("Tell them what you're going to tell them.")
- Note both the topics you'll cover and the amount of time you'll spend.
- Build motivation by showing the benefits.

Middle
Time ______________
- Support your main point. ("Tell them.")
- Limit the number of subpoints to focus attention.
- Provide transitions and internal summaries from point to point.

Ending
Time ______________
- Review. ("Tell them what you've told them.")
- Cycle back to your introduction to demonstrate how far the audience has come through hearing your talk.
- Describe any action the audience should take.
- Create a dramatic image in the audience's mind with a visual or quotation.

Figure 7.5 | Structure of a Presentation. Fill in the blanks to indicate the time to be spent on each segment.

Outline your talk with that time in mind. Unlike readers, listeners can't skim, or skip ahead, or look only at a few pictures, or reread if they've missed something. They are at your mercy to provide a structure and pace for the message that work for them.

Introduction In the introduction, particularly if the audience is not already warmed up to your remarks, build in devices to motivate them and ensure momentum for the content to come. Here are some strategies:

- Pay a compliment to the audience.
- Pose a question.
- Note how the topic relates directly to the audience.
- Detail the benefits the audience will receive from listening.
- Mention a local reference point—a person, place, or favorite saying—familiar to the audience. Their warm feelings toward it may then extend to you.
- Tell a story or anecdote that relates to your main point.
- Show a pertinent cartoon or (cautiously) tell a pertinent joke.

Begin cordially, perhaps with thanks to the person introducing you or to the group that invited you. Establish your connections to that group. In addition, if your audience consists largely of non-native speakers of English, begin your talk in their language. Even if your knowledge of that language is minimal, work with a local counterpart to prepare a courteous opening statement. Such preparation is a sign of politeness that is likely to be well received and to put the audience in a receptive frame of mind for your message. Then continue in English, perhaps handing off to an interpreter who will translate the rest of your talk.

In addition, state at least briefly the context for your remarks, the *why* before the *what*. Note the problem, if there is one, before the solution. Many speakers omit this step, plunging into the details while the audience desperately seeks an overview. Give them the overview.

Middle In the middle, you *tell them*. If your goal is informing, then explain your topic and provide instances. If you aim to persuade the audience, then use examples, expert testimony, statistics, and the like to help them understand and commit to the position you advocate. Take advantage of visuals, both word charts and images, to help them visualize your points, but avoid drowning the audience in overly detailed slides or too many slides. The goal is to achieve a powerful *impression* (see Chapter 6). An excess of information will reduce rather than enhance your impact.

Ending Signal the end with such terms as "finally," "in conclusion," "to wrap this up." Those phrases reenergize the audience if they have bogged down a bit in the middle. So when you say them, be prepared to stop shortly on a strong note:

- Restate the main point to reinforce the audience's understanding.
- Thank the audience for listening.
- Exhort the audience to action.
- Ask for questions.

Have an impressive final slide. If you begin the talk with a slide listing the topics for discussion, you might show it again at the end to mark the audience's progression from new information to now-familiar information and to invite participation in a question-and-answer session. If you're recommending the building of a new hotel, end with a slide showing the architect's drawing or a computer-generated model of it. End, perhaps, with a slide restating your main point. Don't end with a blank screen noting the generic "End of slide show."

Rehearsing

A talk is a *performance,* and only amateurs don't practice. The more serious and influential your talk, the more practice you'll need to build confidence and feel comfortable. Do a run-through at the actual site, if possible. If not, rehearse in a similar room. Speak out loud to become familiar with how you sound in that room. Check your timing to make sure you don't run over—or too much under—the appropriate time. Do a run-through with any technology you'll be using to make sure you understand how it functions, confirm that it does function, and adjust your pacing with it.

Try to enlist others to serve as an audience and then provide comments on your performance. If possible, have someone videotape your rehearsal and perhaps review it with you (see Chapter 9). Use the list in Figure 7.1 to examine your nonverbal behavior, including posture (Do you look natural? Are you blocking the screen? Should you reposition the computer so that you don't block the screen?) and voice (Does your voice drop at the end of sentences so that it's hard to hear final words? Or does your voice rise at the end of sentences in a question-like way?). If you will be using a teleprompter to deliver a scripted presentation, practice so that your gaze falls on the audience, not the teleprompter. If you will work from printed copy, make sure that it is displayed in large type, with wide side and bottom margins, and spacing between the lines. Practice so that you are comfortable reading it. Add marginal notes about timing and pacing as your rehearsal suggests.

Performing

Expect to be nervous before a performance and especially during the first several minutes. To reduce that nervousness, arrive early at the site:

- Make sure the equipment necessary for your talk is working and placed appropriately.
- Arrange furnishings. Do you want to have the chairs in a row? In a U-shape or circle for better interactivity? Are there too many chairs so that you should remove some to the back or side to concentrate the attendees?
- Adjust room temperature—cool is usually better than warm to maintain attention.
- Talk informally with early arrivals who will be participating in the

session. Meeting them may give you a sense of familiarity that will help ease you into the talk.

- Gather your self-confidence and sense of control by being active. Don't just stand around.
- Either in advance or on the spot, learn the names and key interests of at least a sample of members of the audience and use those names and topics to focus the group's attention. Even in a formal presentation, you need to establish membership in the group gathered in the room.

Taking Charge As you begin your talk, let your nervous energy help you be "on." Follow these guidelines:

- Use your posture strategically. If you slouch over a podium or perch on the edge of a table, that positioning sends a signal about casualness that may not be appropriate in a business setting. For a professional appearance, stand tall.
- If you are using electronic presentation software, open with a slide that gives your name and the title of the talk, and use that as the background for your first remarks. Seeing a blank screen, the audience probably won't listen until you show the first slide.
- Keep reading the audience's body language. Monitor facial expressions and restlessness and be flexible in adjusting your remarks to add explanations, define terms, give analogies, ask for questions, and the like.
- Distribute your eye contact equally around the room, not just at a key person or at one side.
- Pace your slides to accommodate the audience's reading and note taking.
- Don't read aloud everything on each slide but emphasize the point the slide shows.
- Welcome pauses as necessary precursors to saying something potentially complex or confusing. A small amount of dead airtime is not always bad.
- Talk to the audience, not the screen. Use a laser pointer to highlight text while you face the audience.
- Remove a visual when you have finished discussing it, but avoid showing the audience a blank but lighted screen.

Participating on a Panel If you are appearing on a panel of several speakers, pay particular attention to the expected length and direction of your remarks. Clarify these constraints with the moderator and, if possible, engage in some preliminary conversation or e-mails with other panelists as you prepare. Do not exceed your time limit because you then put the rest of the panel in jeopardy. Listen to other panelists and integrate their remarks with yours, acknowledging where you may differ or agree, condensing a discussion you had intended to give if another panelist gives it before you. Learn and use the other panelists' names, even if you have met only minutes before the presentation. Referring to someone as "the person at the end there" or pointing, rather than using a name, severely compromises your professionalism.

Distributing Handouts Especially if your talk is controversial, subject to misunderstanding, or delivered in a multilingual context, consider providing a handout—something in hard copy that the audience can take with them. In deciding when to distribute the handout, keep in mind that it will compete with you for the audience's attention. Unless the audience needs to follow it as you speak, reserve its distribution until the end.

The handout may, for example, state an opinion or corporate position so that the audience quotes you accurately, detail the steps in a process that the audience members may later try on their own, offer a translation of your talk, provide a key visual underlying your discussion, summarize your main points, or reproduce your slides in reduced form, usually six to a page. Package any handout attractively, perhaps with a cover page that includes contact information in case a listener wants to get in touch with you after the presentation. Your handout, especially the packet of your slides (sometimes called a *deck*), may also reach audiences who did not attend your talk. With a title page including your name and the logistics of the occasion, and an executive summary (see Appendix B), the deck itself may become a report for senior management and top executives (see Chapter 8). It may also be posted on a Website or an intranet. Prepare your slides so that they will be understandable without your oral commentary on them if you need to accommodate such additional audiences.

Answering Questions You may structure an impromptu presentation entirely in a question-and-answer format. Questions help you determine what the group wants to talk about, what level of detail they need, what explanations and evidence they'll find convincing. With an outlined talk, you can entertain questions during the talk or at the end, as you prefer. If you take questions as you go along, make sure to mark your place so that the questions don't derail your talk or cause you to run out of time before you've solidified your point. In general, with a scripted presentation, you (or a moderator) may request that the audience hold questions until the end. A moderator may introduce a "seed" question while the audience moves from listening mode to talking-and-listening mode.

In working with questions:

- Accommodate to the questioner by listening carefully to understand his or her ideas or concerns.
- Repeat or rephrase the question briefly to show your understanding and to make sure others have heard it. Sort through a comment that may include several questions to answer each in turn.
- Ask for clarification if you don't understand the question. If the questioner's clarification starts to take your talk into a new direction, offer to discuss that issue at a later date.
- Keep your eye on the rest of the audience as well as the questioner to make sure others don't lose interest.
- Ask others in the group to comment on a question you don't know the answer to, if you think that will bring closure rather than serve to instigate a free-for-all discussion. Or take time to think about the question if you're comfortable with the silence and anticipate that the time will produce the answer. Or admit that you don't know and perhaps suggest where the answer may be found or that you'll send the answer later to the questioner.
- Be polite with questioners who seem to be asking a question only to deliver their own speech. But you owe it to the rest of the audience to stop them if their comments are not germane.
- Be fair to a hostile questioner by indicating, perhaps, the need to disagree and agreeing on a statement of that disagreement.

At the end of the session, have the final word: provide a brief summary statement, reiterate the next action step, or, at least, thank the audience.

Branding Your Talk Following these guidelines will help you become an effective presenter. In addition, as you prepare and present, consider how you can *brand* your performance to represent your organization or your personal style. This distinctive quality is hard to measure but often easy for an audience to see. It derives from choices you make about your dress and posture, the background template of your slides if you use them or your decision to stand without them, the words you speak, the visuals you display, among other choices. It also derives from aspects of your delivery that have less to do with deliberate choice and more with who you are: your voice, your energy, your connection with the audience, your *presence*.

SCENARIO

Preparing an International Presentation

Cassandra Bates is the brand manager of a successful breakfast cereal produced by a large American corporation. A professional association of grocery-chain executives in the European Union invited Cassandra's manager, marketing vice president of the cereal manufacturer, to speak about the E.U.'s policy prohibiting importation of foods made from genetically modified (GM) grains. Because the brand Cassandra is responsible for falls under this ban, the vice president suggested her as a substitute speaker, and the association agreed.

Although Cassandra had made numerous presentations to her company's sales staff and had participated in several formal reports to senior management about the brand's status and prospects, she viewed this assignment as much different—and more challenging. To begin with, the audience was external, unlike the inside-the-company groups she had previously addressed. And its members, although all grocery executives, were quite varied, representing different companies and different nations. She had never spoken to a group whose native language was not English. She wasn't even sure how many people would attend or what the setting would be.

When Cassandra asked the vice president for advice on how to prepare her talk in light of these uncertainties, he told her not to worry. "Just focus on the topic," he told her. "Don't worry about the atmospherics. Talk to them as you would your sales staff. They want to hear our views on GM products. We've got lots of research to support our position."

Cassandra followed her manager's suggestion to look into the company's research on GM products, gathering piles of reports that she read at night and on weekends in preparation for the presentation. Two weeks before she was to fly to Brussels for the talk, she had assembled an impressive group of PowerPoint slides to illustrate the point she wanted to make: that scientific research documented the safety of cereals and other foods made from GM grains. She wrote a lengthy script of the talk she would give as she showed the slides and interpreted the information for her audience.

She asked both the vice president and two of her colleagues to review the script and slides. The vice president congratulated her on the thoroughness of her work. One of her fellow brand managers raised questions about the formality of the presentation and the amount of information her slides conveyed. Cassandra responded that she would rather be overprepared than underprepared. The other colleague asked Cassandra several questions: How many people would be there? What sort of talk would they expect? Would they understand the scientific information? If they were experts, could Cassandra respond adequately? Where would the talk be given?

Cassandra admitted she didn't really know the answers to those questions, but she felt she didn't have time to find out. She was due to fly to Brussels that night, and the talk was already prepared. She thanked her colleagues, packed her laptop and script, and headed for the airport.

She had a free day in Brussels to accommodate jet lag before giving her talk at 10:00 A.M. the next day. When she arrived at her hotel, she phoned the managing director of the association and arranged to meet him at the conference center late in the afternoon to look over the room and discuss the talk.

"It's a small group," the managing director told her as they stood in the tiny room where the group would meet the next morning. "Ten or twelve people," he added. "They like to have a good dialogue, so you can talk for 15 minutes and then just get into the questions."

"I don't think so," he answered when Cassandra asked about a screen for projecting the slides. "We could probably get one, but we weren't expecting anything formal like that."

Cassandra went back to her hotel to think about what she would do.

Questions for Discussion

1. What would you advise Cassandra to do? Review her options. For example,
   - She can go ahead with the talk as planned, hoping a screen can be provided by the morning.
   - She can rework her script into an outline from which she can talk informally.

- She can produce her slides on paper to hand out as she reads her script.
- She can start fresh, taking key points from her script and then posing possible issues for the audience to discuss.

Are there other options? What are the advantages and disadvantages of each?

2. What might Cassandra have done earlier in the preparation process to avoid the problem she is confronting? How could she have found out more about the context and setting of her talk so she could have prepared a more appropriate presentation?
3. Was Cassandra wrong to follow the vice president's suggestions? How could she have managed the political situation of trying to find out more about the talk without putting herself in an uncomfortable position with her organizational superior?
4. Should Cassandra have sought advice from her colleagues earlier in her presentation preparation?
5. What information about the talk should Cassandra have had, from whatever sources, before preparing it?

CHAPTER

Creating the Communication Product: Emphasis on Writing

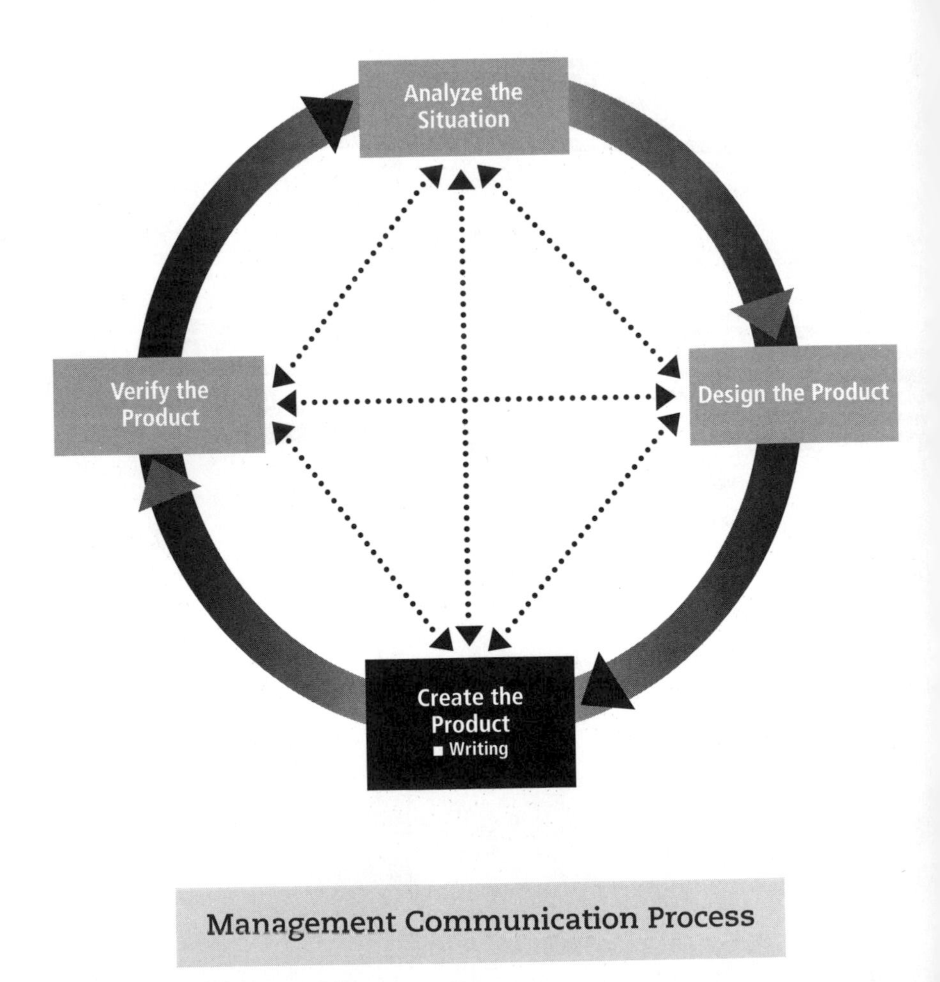

The situations discussed in Chapter 7 foreground good speaking skills. But most require some writing as well. The communication products discussed in this chapter foreground writing, but they are often integrated with conversations, meetings, and presentations. The chapter starts with managerial correspondence, including memos, letters, and e-mail. In these you maintain personal and organizational relationships, encourage action, influence people, and create a permanent record. To do so you write within the box of conventions for that format (see Appendix B), although conventions for e-mail are less well established. In their correspondence, or in longer self-standing documents, managers also write two important genres of documents that help accomplish organizational goals: a proposal and a report. The chapter ends with a brief look at each of these.

Memos

As a major communication tool within an organization, memos accomplish such routine tasks as making announcements, distributing the agendas and minutes of meetings, describing policies and procedures, requesting information and responding to such requests, and issuing brief reports. Increasingly, memos circulate on e-mail systems. But you may need to create a memo on paper to signal special importance in a message, convey a difficult or controversial message, or serve as a covering note to a print document like a report, handbook, or brochure.

Gaining the Audience's Attention

To create a memo, first fill in the blanks of the standard header, generally preprinted on a company form or in your e-mail system, usually in the following order (see Appendix B). An e-mail system will automatically complete the *date* and *from* slots.

Date:
From:
To:
Subject:

In addition, the header may include a notation for those who should receive copies (cc). Pay particular attention to the *to* and *subject* lines.

To Select your audience carefully, both those who will receive your memo directly and those who will receive copies. While you may write to just one person, you often address a set of people—for example, members of a company division, participants on a project team, or attendees at a meeting. In doing so, avoid a round-up-the-usual-suspects approach. Adhere to any company policies about who should receive memos on certain topics. In addition, weigh the political implications of the distribution list. Sometimes, messages sent to peers and managers reflect the writer's self-promotion more than the pursuit of an organizational goal. Write only to those people who really need the message (while not slighting anyone), and only when they really need it, not just when you want to send it. A reputation as someone who writes only when necessary will increase your likelihood of being read seriously.

Subject Use the subject line—the memo's title—to gain audience attention and market your message. Announce the topic in a way that makes clear what the reader should do about it:

- FYI: 3rd quarter results [*no action needed*]
- New Benefits Policy Effective 1 July [*read to understand and comply*]
- Agenda for 14 December meeting [*read as a way to prepare for the meeting*]
- Draft Agenda for 14 December for your approval [*read closely, send approval or comments*]

8

If you have two different messages to deliver to the same reader, use two different memos, each with an attention-getting heading. The reader may assign a different priority to each, store each in a different project folder, or forward each to a different reader for further action.

Designing the Message

In designing your memo, focus on being brief and modular. Try to limit yourself to one page. If you need more pages, consider creating a one-page covering memo that forecasts the message segments that follow. In addition, make sure your memo is timely, sent at the right time to meet a current need.

Introduction Open with a short paragraph, maybe only one sentence, that motivates the reader to enter your message *now*. Provide the memo's context and main point:

- What action or understanding you seek from the reader.
- Why you selected this reader or readers to receive the message.
- Why you—rather than someone else—wrote the memo (your role in the organization or on a team may make this obvious, but clarify if it's not).
- Why you are sending the memo today, rather than yesterday or tomorrow.

Attached for your review by Tuesday 15 July is the latest draft of our business plan for expansion into Montréal.

I am writing in response to your request for a listing of Olympic-size hotel swimming pools in the Northwest.

Middle Divide the middle of your message into short modules, including paragraphs and lists. In addition,

- use headings to label the modules and ease skimming.
- include or attach visuals as appropriate.
- if the memo responds to a request, structure your information to match that request.
- use attachments for detailed discussion.

Ending End by noting any action or decision the reader should take. You might also include contact information for someone (you or someone else) who could provide more information if needed.

Branding Your Memos

Because memos are internal documents, use insider's language and abbreviations common in your organization or profession. You can also omit the small talk and politeness statements required in more formal letters to outsiders. But even though memos are brief and often fairly routine, take advantage of them as an opportunity to establish yourself and your message (see Chapters 5 and 6).

In general, answer these questions before you send your memo:

- *Can I tighten the text?* Look for ways to reduce formality and condense by cutting cumbersome phrases ("Based on a thorough review of all available evidence, this writer recommends . . ."), by shortening sentences, or by creating more paragraphs and lists.

- *Is the message clear?* Focus on the central point. You know more than you need to say in this memo, and that extraneous information will only dilute, not strengthen, your message. Cut to the point.
- *Will my reader understand?* Review your language (Would the reader understand this term?) and the amount of detail you present. In addition, review the impression your memo creates. Does it show you in a good light, but in a way that avoids mere self-promotion and serves the reader and the organization?

Letters

Letters, like memos, are a form of correspondence through which you start or maintain a relationship. Unlike memos, letters usually are reserved for correspondence between individuals or between an organization and an individual, not within an organization. As they are more formal and traditional than memos, letters also adhere to more complex conventions, and those conventions differ internationally (see Appendix B for the format of U.S. letters). The convenience and speed of e-mail mean that an ever-smaller percentage of day-to-day managerial communication finds its way into letters. But sometimes only a letter will do. Letters

- have a certain weight and authority.
- foster the delivery of information, especially legal or financial information, that is complex and may be subject to misunderstanding.
- are private (unlike e-mail, which is easily monitored and less secure).
- seem more sensitive than e-mail for messages tinged with emotion, like condolences or thanks.

Gaining the Audience's Attention

Center the letter on the reader. That means you ingratiate yourself with the reader from the start and take the reader's point of view. Especially when asking a favor, consider how you can show your knowledge of the reader and enhance the reader's self-esteem to encourage a positive response to your request:

> Having read with pleasure—and profit—your column in the *Journal* every Monday, I'm writing to invite you to give a keynote address in our orientation program for new financial analysts.

Similarly, be careful to save face for the reader if, for example, you're responding to someone who is wrong about a situation or product. Internally, you want to start by saying, "You dummy." Instead, be sensitive to how the mistake or misperception might have occurred and start with that understanding before moving into the correction:

> I'm sorry that you found our instructions for filing a 1202 claim confusing and had to spend all that time on them. I'll try to clarify here some of the issues you raise in your 12 December letter.

Designing the Message

Follow the same three-part design (introduction, middle, ending) in a letter as in a memo. The introduction and ending of a letter, however, respond to different politeness conventions befitting the letter's outsider audience. Those conventions vary greatly internationally, something to keep in mind when you write (and read) international correspondence. Letters in the United States, like U.S. business in general, tend to be direct, an approach some readers find brusque. Acknowledge previous correspondence and explain why you are writing. Then use short paragraphs to detail your message, although you will probably not use headings for them, as you might in a memo. Try to keep letters to one page. Lawyers, major producers of letters, often write longer ones, but readers are better served if they can see the beginning and end of the letter on one page.

Branding Your Letters

When you write as a spokesperson for your organization, follow recommended practices. Imitate the approach of letters in a file devoted to such situations or a template in your word processing system. Writing within the box of such conventions

- reinforces a corporate image.
- speeds up the writing process.
- controls the quality of the text.
- minimizes inconsistencies when several writers create letters.

Readers may object, however, to entirely canned letters. Within the conventions, create a letter in your own voice, which will have a clearer ring of authenticity. Avoid in particular "letterly" language:

Letterly	More Direct
Please be advised by this correspondence that	I'm writing to . . .
We wish to advise you that	[omit; just begin]
The undersigned	I
I am in receipt of your letter of recent date	In response to your [date] letter
As per your request	In response to your request

Establish your own voice in language reflecting the 21st century.

E-Mail

For reasons that are well known, e-mail is the management communication medium of choice today. It allows you to carry on a conversation in writing and to write more interactively than in a memo or letter. It's particularly suited to fast communication internationally and has helped blur the borders among people within organizations and between audiences internal and external to the organization. But because it's a young medium, conventions for using it are only gradually being codified. Many of the conventions for creating effective memos apply as well to e-mail, so keep those in mind as you write. In addition, here are some further guidelines that should help you reap the benefits of e-mail without falling prey to its very real dangers. Unfortunately, people jeopardize their career every day by sending inappropriate e-mail.

Gaining the Audience's Attention

At the beginning of an e-mail correspondence, make sure you and your audience share not only the same technology but also the same view of e-mail's appropriateness to different situations. Some people rightly feel e-mail is appropriate only for the routine transfer of uncomplicated information; others see it as a quick way to send any kind of message. Find out your audience's views. In addition, the interactivity inherent in an e-mail exchange often leads to a perception that questions and ideas are open for further discussion. E-mail can encourage quarreling and argument, unlike traditional memos and letters, which seem to have greater finality. Your comfort level with such openness also needs to match that of your audience. Especially in a team project, clarify early on the protocol and limits for e-mail discussions (see Chapter 11).

As in a memo, use the header to sell your message, particularly the distribution list and subject line.

To The ease of electronic delivery often tempts writers to expand a distribution list. Resist. Especially for any message that is more than a mere announcement, severely limit the number of recipients. In a group or Listserv discussion, don't automatically respond to everyone. It's often best if the person posting a query or idea receives responses individually and compiles them into one message. Before you send your message, review the "to" line once more to make sure that potential recipients are the right ones and that the addresses are correct. A small oversight, like having a "Steve" in your address book who is not the right "Steve" to receive this message, can have calamitous, unintended consequences.

Subject Never settle for a default subject line ("Re: Your mail"). Instead, keeping in mind the speed and timeliness of e-mail, craft a message-specific heading. The heading alone in an index may give a busy reader a needed answer without requiring the message to be opened right away:

Re: Houston Meeting Cancelled
Re: Genitor Accepts Proposal!
Re: Product Specs Completed

Place key words early in the subject line (see Chapter 5). When a change of topic occurs in a series of messages, rephrase the subject line to alert respondents to that change.

Designing the Message

Unlike a memo, which generally moves directly from the heading into the text, e-mails sometimes include a personal greeting, usually on the first line ("Hi," or "Hi, Jill," or "Jill"). Where more formality is appropriate, especially internationally, that greeting may look like the opening to a letter: "Dear Mr. Smith." Your own preferences, and the preferences of your audience (whose e-mails may just start with the text), will dictate your approach.

State your main point in the first line of the first paragraph. The frequency of e-mail exchanges means that you don't need as much context building in each e-mail as you do in memos, but provide enough for clarity. To keep down the number of subsequent messages, try to anticipate and answer the respondent's questions in one good message. As a test for brevity and clarity, think of your e-mail as being read by someone who is charging you by the minute to read it and frame a response. In addition:

- Keep messages short—even shorter than a typical memo, because readers don't like to scroll.
- If you need to cover more than one screen, use an opening statement that forecasts what's to come ("This message briefly outlines the draft's main points and differences between this version and the version we discussed on 12 June." "Sorry about the length of this posting, but please keep scrolling through the following three points.").
- Divide your message into short modules, especially short paragraphs and lists.
- Unless preservation of the full text is important for future reference, paraphrase or select highlights from the message you are responding to rather than reproducing it.
- In quoting a previous message, put your text first, then your correspondent's, carefully differentiating each.

Branding Your E-Mail

As a medium of communication, e-mail accommodates a wide variety of message types, so adjust your expression to match your relationship to the audience and the dictates of a particular circumstance. The casual voice of conversation is often appropriate—language that is too formal may strike readers as odd even in a serious business context. But e-mail, unlike conversation, does create a permanent record. That record may not matter much in routine exchanges about having lunch or scheduling a meeting. But for important contexts and documents (and it's a test of your managerial judgment to know which these are), think what your e-mail will look like if the recipient prints it. Consider writing off-line, proofreading, and perhaps having others review the text before you send it online. If your message is lengthy, consider sending it as an attachment. Refer to the attachment in the body of your message and check before sending to make sure you have indeed attached the document, and that it is the right document.

Managing Your E-Mail

Deciding what to put into an e-mail message, determining the right pace for an e-mail exchange, and sorting and filing the multiple messages you receive and send via e-mail are tasks that have probably become major elements in your day (and, often, nights and weekends).

Going Public with Your Message In creating your message, make sure that no one (including you) would be harmed if it were made public. E-mail is, realistically, a public medium, and messages can be legitimately read by employers and the government. In addition, your audience may also easily forward your message to unintended readers, notwithstanding the dire warning against such a practice that some corporate e-mail systems automatically attach to every message. One CEO sent a chastising and angry e-mail to 400 managers, equating empty spaces in the company parking lot with lack of worker motivation and productivity and threatening vague if severe sanctions unless managers made their workers shape up. The message, however, was leaked and posted on Yahoo! Its tone surprised thousands of readers, including investors and analysts, and the valuation of the company dropped 22 percent in three days. In addition, even though you may delete messages, others may be able to retrieve them. So avoid e-mail for private messages. You can't assume that you and the intended recipient will be the exclusive readers.

Pacing While timing is critical in all communication (see Chapter 4), you have to time an e-mail correspondence not only to the external events that require communication but also to the pace at which you and your correspondent expect messages from each other. Some people are comfortable with long silences between messages, whereas others find even an hour or two of silence unnerving or rude. So in your individual exchanges as well as exchanges on a team consider developing specific guidelines for the pace of a discussion ("Let's check in every Wednesday and at other times as necessary.").

The intense interactivity of e-mail also leads to a condition some researchers call "the long goodbye." Oral conversations end in a series of fairly predictable moves, both nonverbal (like looking at the clock or tidying a stack of papers) and verbal—summing up, appealing to an external circumstance, exchanging a pleasantry ("Great to see you!"), or noting something in the future ("Let's get together again soon."). But a similar distancing can be more difficult in e-mail, which lacks the same context clues. People keep writing back and forth ("Received your message." "Thanks for letting me know you received the message." "No problem."). Instead, just trust that an e-mail system will automatically let you know if a message bounced. Or engage a system function that requests a confirmation of receipt if you tend to worry. In addition, consider using the subject line ("FYI" generally means no response is needed) and ending ("No reply needed." "Unless I hear from you, I'll assume this is ok.") to sign off on an exchange courteously but briefly.

Sorting and Filing Prioritize your e-mail reading and writing as you do other tasks (see Chapter 5):

- If you're not going to be reading e-mail for a while, let your correspondents know that fact, perhaps using your system's autoresponse function.
- Read an entire index of new messages to determine which ones (usually those addressed only to you rather than ones from a Listserv) are most important and start your detailed reading with those.
- Read the last message in a series from the same sender before you read earlier ones because the last message may correct or suggest that you ignore an earlier statement.
- Sort messages to determine the order and speed of your response.
- Read online, but keep paper handy to jot down points to which you need to respond.
- Print only those messages that require further processing as paper.

Periodically look through your active in-box to delete messages that were of only momentary interest, move some into folders for future reference, and check on messages that may have fallen through the cracks of your attention. In general, keep a wary eye on your e-mail habits. It's easy to consume large quantities of your day reading and responding to e-mail. Some of that time is certainly necessary and effective in achieving your communication goals. But some time on the screen may only postpone your getting to work.

Proposals

Using the format of a memo, a letter, or an e-mail, you may write two important genres of managerial communication: a proposal and a report (see Chapter 5 for more about genre). You may also give each of these genres full-dress treatment as a longer, self-standing document (see Appendix B). The conventions of the genre help you select and structure the content of your message. This section briefly discusses proposals; the next discusses final reports. Both are significant as you develop a repertoire of genres that interrelate to accomplish your personal and organizational goals.

A proposal is an offer to provide a product or service or to do some kind of work to solve a problem. In a *solicited* proposal, you respond to someone's request for your work (the "request for proposal" or RFP). An *unsolicited* proposal derives from your own initiative. You have, for example, an idea for speeding up the collection of receivables. You then suggest your idea to someone who can profit from it. As a rule, a solicited proposal sells the answer, whereas an unsolicited proposal explains the problem—and then sells the answer. The length and design of proposals differ widely, but the structure presented in Figure 8.1 should help you start your planning.

In writing a proposal, follow these guidelines:

- Develop one core idea and make sure it governs every part of the proposal. Don't be afraid to repeat it ("Our benefits management program serves both you and your employees.").
- Think in the audience's terms. Avoid a list of "I want" sentences. State features of your solution as benefits to the audience ("Your employees will welcome our easy-to-read reports." "Daily reporting features keep all records current." "Careful monitoring of claims and payments saves you money.").
- Use the audience's language, particularly repeating any key terms or concepts in the request for your proposal.
- Use the present tense for general descriptions and the future for actions in the future. You and the reader both know that future steps depend on acceptance of the proposal, so you don't need the conditional (The work *would be done* . . .).

Introduction

Summarizes your proposed activity by stressing benefits to the reader. Provides the context by briefly restating the problem (if the proposal is solicited) or establishing the problem's background and urgency (if unsolicited). Provides an overview of the content and plan of the proposal for a wide readership.

Statement of Problem

Identifies the problem necessitating the proposed work, with enough detail to make the problem clear to the reader. Provides a review of relevant literature, if that is needed to establish the significance or dimensions of the problem.

Objective(s)

Lists the specific, measurable outcomes you plan to accomplish. Explains the solution you will propose. In a research proposal, shows that your work will contribute to the theme established by a funding agency, client, or sponsor.

Method or Activities

Explains either how you will implement your solution (if the solution is known) or how you will conduct research to support your hypothesis about the solution (if it is unknown). Ties the activities directly to your objectives. Convinces the reader that your approach is reasonable, suited to your resources in people and facilities, likely to succeed, and better than the competitors'. May include a review of literature to show how the proposed approach derives from but improves on that of other workers, and is innovative and distinctive. Notes compliance with any federal, state, or local laws in undertaking the work. Indicates your procedures for ensuring quality control.

Management

In a collaborative proposal effort, shows how the team will be coordinated, scheduled, and monitored. Profiles the key staff along with the extent of their participation in the proposed project (extended biographies may be included in an appendix).

Schedule

Places your implementation or research activities on a time line. Convinces the audience that the time line is realistic. Serves as the proposal at a glance.

Justification

Answers the question "Why you?" Provides your track record of relevant accomplishments. Assures the reader that adequate staff and facilities are available to carry out the project as outlined. Describes laboratory or field sites, specialized equipment, and computer and other information systems matched to the tasks. Convinces the audience that the project is worth doing.

Figure 8.1 | Typical Content of Segments of a Proposal

Budget

Assigns monetary values to all activities or resources mentioned in the proposal. Often read first as, in effect, the quantitative abstract of the proposal. Divides the total budget into categories.

Figure 8.1 Cont. | Typical Content of Segments of a Proposal

Final Reports

A *report* is an account of some activity and what it adds up to, and *reporting* is a key managerial task. A report may aim mainly to inform the reader (as in a summary of account activities over the last year) or to persuade (as in a report recommending the expansion of the company's business into Montréal, Canada). Because reports differ greatly in purpose, audience, and structure, you'll have to adjust your design to the situation at hand (see Appendix B). Figure 8.2 presents a series of questions to consider in creating the final report on an investigation.

In general, in writing a long report addressing multiple readers you should

- provide several points of access to different parts that match different reader interests, including headings, a table of contents, and perhaps cover letters that direct different users to different sections.
- brief all readers, no matter what their particular interests, in an executive summary (see Appendix B) and general introduction.
- build in redundancy so everyone will read the main points even if no one reads straight through.
- give the answer up front unless you anticipate resistance or your audience prefers an indirect approach. Avoid simply reporting on what you did in the order in which you did it.

Introduction
- Who asked me to look into this?
- Why did they ask our team or me?
- Why did they see this as a problem?
- Who else knows about this and has written about it (review of literature)?
- Has anything happened like this in the company or as recorded in the literature before?
- If so, what was the outcome then?
- What limits did I have in solving this (budget, time, overlap with someone else's responsibility)?
- What priority does this have in the company?
- What was I specifically asked to do?
- Are there any hidden agendas?

Methods
- Where did I look for information?
- What chief areas did I study?
- Whom did I talk with?
- What did I read?
- What surveys or observations did I make?
- What tools or machines did I use?

Results
- What results did I obtain from my work? What did I find out?
- Are these results accurate? How do I know?
- Are these results valid? How do I know?

Discussion
- Do the results show any trends? Short term? Long term?
- What do they add up to?
- How do they relate to other findings?
- Do the conclusions match my assignment?
- Have I overlooked anything I was asked to do?
- So what? In the reader's terms, and the organization's terms, what does all this matter? Future work?

Figure 8.2 | Structuring Information for the Final Report on an Investigation

SCENARIO

Producing an Electronic Report

Between her junior and senior years in college, Jennifer Krontos worked as a summer intern at a regional brokerage firm in Atlanta. Because she enjoyed the work, she decided to seek a career in the investment industry. When she graduated, the firm offered her a full-time position as assistant to Suzanne Lubecki, the chief investment officer. Jennifer accepted because she admired Suzanne and saw her as a potential mentor and because the job promised to be flexible and therefore a good introduction to various career paths within investments. Impressed with Jennifer's dual major in finance and communication, Suzanne assigned her to design and produce a daily report for analysts and brokers.

On Jennifer's first day on the job, Suzanne outlined her thinking. "Because of our acquisitions, we have offices from the Florida Keys to the suburbs of Washington. I need to make them feel they're part of the team, and I want them to work from the same script—to understand and follow my investment guidance so the firm really takes on a single image."

"The brand," Jennifer said.

"Exactly. I need all the analysts and brokers to be on the same page, so the advice we provide to all our clients makes us distinctive and gives us a competitive edge. I know we do good work in identifying opportunities and in following Southern companies that the big Wall Street outfits overlook. We just have to communicate the quality of our work consistently. That's going to be your job, Jennifer—putting together a daily report that summarizes general market conditions, gives my slant on them, and highlights our recommendations. Take a look at what we send out now, and talk to some of the brokers in the offices here and out in the branches to find out what they need. Let's talk in a week or so about what you think the new product should be. I'd like to get it up and running by July."

Jennifer found that two forms of communication went to all the firm's brokers and analysts: the "Long-Term Winners for Long-Term Investors" list of recommended stocks that was updated as needed and mailed in paper form, and Suzanne's frequent e-mails on specific market actions and recommendations. To gauge the effectiveness of these, she made phone calls to brokers at each of the firm's offices and interviewed the analysts who worked under Suzanne in Atlanta. What she learned was instructive but not consistent:

- Some, but not all, of the brokers forwarded copies of the "Long-Term Winners" list to their clients. Some even forwarded Suzanne's e-mails, a practice that made Jennifer nervous since these messages were meant to be internal.
- Most found Suzanne's e-mails helpful in designing investment strategies for their clients, but a few reported that they considered her advice erratic and, as one said, "too self-congratulatory, as if Suzanne is the only person who understands the market."
- Some of the brokers whose small, locally oriented firms had been merged into the Atlanta operation still resented being part of a bigger, regional brokerage and resisted Suzanne's direction and effort to create uniform investment strategies. "We're not General Motors," one of them told Jennifer. "We need to tailor our advice to the people we know best, not some hot-shot analyst in Atlanta."
- While all the brokers were on the firm's e-mail system, they varied greatly in their use of it. A number of them said they never looked at their e-mail until the end of the day.

Two days before she was supposed to make her recommendations, Jennifer asked Suzanne if they could have a brainstorming session to review some of the issues. To focus the discussion, Jennifer wrote a one-page memo:

Tentative recommendations

1. E-mail message, sent at 8:30 A.M. every day the markets are open, to all analysts and brokers, with the subject line "Market Report."
2. Elimination of the paper list of "Long-Term Winners for Long-Term Investors," with an updated version of that list to be attached to each daily message.
3. Reduction or elimination of Suzanne's special e-mail messages; all communications to be made through the daily Market Report to avoid confusion and information overload.

Issues to resolve

1. Security—should the Market Report be strictly internal? Some brokers now forward it to clients attached to e-mails. Is a statement about this

being proprietary and meant for internal use adequate to prevent forwarding? Should the report be written so it can be circulated—something a few brokers think would be helpful because they could make their clients feel they're on the "inside"?

2. Tone—how can we make the message lively and get everyone's attention but at the same time make it professional and serious and meet any legal concerns? We don't want brokers to be churning accounts to take advantage of hot recommendations, but we want them to read this and use it.
3. "From" line: who's the report from? Suzanne Lubecki, Chief Investment Officer? Or should it be sent under the firm's name to give it maximum authority and branding power?
4. Length—an e-mail should be pretty short, but sometimes we may need to do a lot of analysis and explanation and maybe include charts, tables, and so forth. Add more attachments for that? But will people read a long e-mail?
5. Paper—should we also send a paper version to everyone, or should we ask them to print it out? It would be good to have a complete file of all these reports so brokers can review them. If it's only on e-mail, some might delete the message after they read it
6. Title—is "Market Report" too bland and generic? Is there a better name that really emphasizes our brand and gets attention?
7. How do we get everyone to read the message right away, every day, before the markets open? Some people still ignore their e-mail until the late afternoon. We have to be sure they look at the Market Report first thing every day.

"Well, your unresolved issues exceed your tentative conclusions by two to one," Suzanne told Jennifer as they began their meeting. "But you've raised the right points—let's see if we can work through these together."

Questions for Discussion

1. Is Jennifer's strategy of getting her manager's buy-in on the issues correct? Does she risk undermining her own credibility by bringing forward so many unresolved issues just two days before her recommendations are due? What would you suggest she do?

2. Has Jennifer done enough research? What else might she do to strengthen her recommendations? What further information should she seek?
3. Do you agree or disagree with Jennifer's tentative conclusions? Why or why not?
4. How would you resolve the issues she presents: security, tone, "from" line, length, paper, title, and the best way to get everyone to read the message at the beginning of the day. Explain your recommendations by analyzing the new reporting system for audience, purpose, media, and timing.

CHAPTER

Verifying the Communication Product

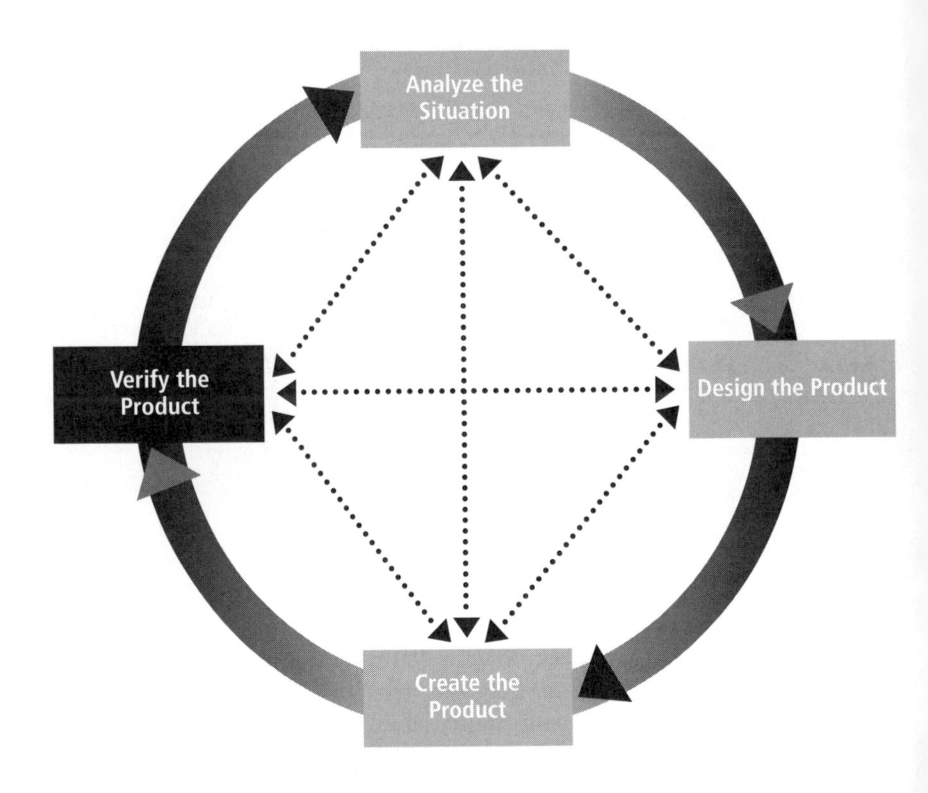

Management Communication Process

Although you can't know the success of a message until the receiver responds—buys your product, agrees with your idea, complies with your request—you can increase the likelihood of success by verifying the communication product before you present it. Verification includes editing: attention to punctuation, spelling, word choice, and mechanics. But it is more than editing—a broad process aimed at increasing the ability of the communication product to achieve your intended results.

Take an External Perspective

Verification requires you to take an external perspective on your work, to look freshly at what you've done, as if someone else had done it. Step outside your role as the producer of the communication product and read the draft document or outline of the presentation as if you were on the receiving end. Ask:

- Does it make a clear point?
- Is that point adequately supported?
- Are counterarguments or alternative approaches properly dealt with?
- Do the words, numbers, and pictures make sense?
- Do you know what to do next—what is expected of you as the receiver?

Ask tough questions that the audience may not think of but that may affect their reaction. Be sure to

- check spelling and punctuation.
- cut words to sharpen expression, or substitute words to enhance meaning.
- add columns of numbers to make sure the totals are correct.
- scrutinize visuals to be sure they're understandable.
- question generalizations and assertions to see if more support is needed.
- test if the document conforms to all conventions—e.g., that if it's a letter it follows your company's letter format.

Verify While and After You Write

Verification is a continuous process because you question yourself as you write. While it's hard to write and at the same time look critically at what you're writing, it's important to cultivate a dual perspective that allows you to see what you're doing and ask questions about it while you're doing it.

But in producing any business document, you reach a point when you have a final draft that you can step back from and look at from an outside perspective. With a written document, it's fairly easy to identify that point. If the document is an e-mail, final verification comes before you hit "Send." With paper, it's when you're ready to put the letter in an envelope or carry the memo to someone's office.

Oral presentations are different. Because they don't exist until delivered, you have to verify oral presentations by looking at the slides or script. But since voice, gestures, and timing are so critical to success in oral presentations, you should also verify the run-through, the preview, or the practice session. It's hard to be simultaneously the speaker, the listener, and a third-party editor, but with experience you can learn to do that. You can also get help from a colleague in verifying an oral presentation in its preview mode.

Verify Against Your Standards

Use two standards to verify the draft:

- Your analysis of the communication situation.
- The outline you created to guide the document or talk.

Through analysis (see Chapters 3 and 4), you identified what, to whom, how, and when you are communicating. As you verify, go back to these items and make sure your communication product addresses each point as you intended. The outline you made following your analysis (see Chapter 6) embodies the choices you made and shows the order of presentation. Does your draft leave out anything? Add something? Move a section? Leave a major point undeveloped?

Often in drafting a document, you make a decision, perhaps unconsciously, to add, subtract, or move. You may do so for a good reason. But as you verify, check to see if you've made changes and then ask if they improve the document or happened simply because you forgot something. It's normal to make changes from your original outline as you write, but be sure you understand why. And be sure any changes make the document stronger than it would be if you had faithfully followed the original outline.

Verify the Information

The information you use should meet the standards shown in Figure 9.1. Your information is *comprehensible* when the audience is capable of understanding it. Avoid unnecessary complexity. Use information that enlightens rather than obscures, and don't try to impress your audience with fancy statistics or bizarre facts.

Your information is *credible* when it derives from careful observation or accepted authorities (including yourself) and can be independently verified (see Chapter 3).

Your information is *timely* when it provides the latest evidence for decision making. In a 24/7 environment in which information is available around the clock, use electronic technology to access the latest available information, but exercise caution about the source of information found on Websites.

Your information is *adequate* when it serves the purpose that you and your audience share in the communication product. Provide enough information to support your argument or analysis.

Your information is *relevant* when it relates directly to the matter at

Information you use in management communications should be:	
Comprehensible	understandable to your audience
Credible	both accurate and reliable
Timely	as up to date as possible
Adequate	enough to support your analysis or argument
Relevant	directly related to the matter at hand

Figure 9.1 | Guidelines for Verifying Information

hand. Otherwise acceptable information may simply be irrelevant. Managers are naturally inclined to include whatever information they spent time and energy developing. But relevance needs to be the test.

As you verify the draft communication product, make one run-through for all numbers and quotations, ignoring at the moment the way in which the information is expressed and concentrating on the information itself. Verify the information as if it were free standing.

Make sure you have cited both numbers and quotations accurately. Go back to the original sources to verify them. And be sure the numbers add up. Explain anomalies—unexpected patterns, data that don't appear to make sense, odd spikes. If profit rises dramatically in the second quarter—a fact that would jump out at the audience—explain why. Perhaps second-quarter sales are historically high, or maybe the company recognizes investment gains that quarter. If your audience might question an issue, anticipate that question and answer it in advance.

Verify the Expression

With your analysis and outline as standards, verify the message at three levels: effectiveness, efficiency, and conventionality. The issues for each level are summarized in Figure 9.2.

Effectiveness means doing the right thing, whereas efficiency means doing things right. When you assess the *effectiveness* of a draft document or presentation preview, look at big-picture issues: Does this memo (or other product) accomplish what I want for its intended audience? When you assess its *efficiency,* consider whether it does so in the most direct, economical, clear way. When you assess *conventionality,* look at the standards of language and usage expected in your culture, business, and particular company—the details of grammar, punctuation, and style that your audience assumes.

Begin at the Top

Inexperienced writers tend to begin verifying at the lowest level, checking for grammar and spelling. That's important and relatively easy work, but it should come at the end of the verification process. Begin at the top, the *effectiveness* of the draft. Then move on to *efficiency,* whether your draft does its job the best way. After you have satisfied yourself about the effectiveness and efficiency of your draft, look at mechanical and sty-

Level 3: Effectiveness

- Answer the audience's key question—what's the point?
- Show the audience the context, how the subject at hand affects them.
- Build modules of support for the main point, asking and answering questions, making and defending claims, providing explanations and definitions.
- Distinguish the new from the familiar, and start with the familiar.
- Engage and sustain the audience's attention.
- Help the reader understand and remember.

Level 2: Efficiency

- Adjust the length and depth of the product to the task and to your credibility with this audience.
- Streamline and check information—is it comprehensible, credible, timely, adequate, and relevant?
- Design for access through hierarchy and parallelism.
- Connect the supporting modules by making the moves the audience expects, either moves you've taught them to expect or those standard for the genre.
- Signal relationships—forecast statements, headings, connecting words, repetition, layout, type, color.
- Make smart choices between visual and textual display.

Level 1: Conventionality

- Adjust the level of language (word choice) to the audience.
- Conform to conventions and any applicable style guide.
- Focus on sentence construction.
- Review all verbs—make them work, keep them precise.
- Proofread for spelling, punctuation, mechanics.
- Proofread again.

Figure 9.2 | Checklist for Verifying Expression

listic issues: the line-by-line, word-by-word proofreading that people mean when they talk about editing. As you review the draft document for effectiveness and efficiency, don't ignore spelling or other mechanical errors. Correct all errors when you find them. But don't take your first pass through the draft for the purpose of checking on mechanics. Save that until last because you'll waste time if, later, a section you edited closely has to be deleted.

Effectiveness: The Big Picture

On your first pass, focus on the big picture: does this document or talk do what I want it to do for the audience I have in mind? Issues of goals, outcomes, and audience are paramount. Check to see that you highlighted your main point, supported it with appropriate information, and presented it so the audience understands both it and its significance.

Efficiency: The Best Way

When you're satisfied with the big picture, take another pass through the document or talk to see if you've presented your idea in the best way. Focus on parts rather than the whole. Assess whether you've provided too much or too little supporting information, whether you've made sections and paragraphs clear and connected them appropriately, and whether you've signaled relationships and distributed information strategically between text and visuals (see Chapter 6). Continue to think of your purpose and audience, but concentrate particularly on how the parts of the whole work together to make your point to that audience.

Conventionality: Meeting Expectations

Your audience expects you to express yourself according to the standards you share. On the last pass through the draft document or talk, pay attention to spelling, grammar, word choice, and the conventions of presentation for the type of product you're creating (e.g., letter format or informal talk without visuals). Meet expectations by distancing yourself from the draft and pretending someone else produced it. Don't rely on the spell-checking and grammar alerts built into your word-processing package, which are notoriously fallible (usually "there" will pass muster even when you mean "their"). Go through the draft word by word, line by line, and avoid being lulled by the sound of your own voice. Try to be someone else—your own worst critic. (See Appendix A for specific advice on word choice, sentence structure, and punctuation.)

Brand It: Back to the Big Picture

Through at least three passes, you're sure the big picture is right, the parts work well together, and you've followed all conventions. Now take one more look, this time to see if the document or talk carries your *brand*.

Does it sound and look like the best memo, the best proposal, the best presentation? Is it distinctive? Is it *you?* You want the audience to say, "That's the kind of work we expect from her" or "That's what he does so well."

Getting and Giving Help in Verifying

Because verifying requires you to role-play, to be both the audience and a disinterested third party, you can improve the quality of verification by asking someone else to help. Getting help and giving help are routine, expected parts of your job as a manager.

Using Others to Help Verify Your Communication Product

Ask a colleague or friend to read your draft. Specify the level of editing you want. Seek suggestions for improvement—and accept them graciously, even if you finally decide not to adopt them. Particularly in verifying an oral product—the run-through of a presentation, for example—the perspectives of one or more people not involved in the work itself can be hugely helpful.

Of course, you have to do your part. Explain the context—what you're doing, for whom, and why. Describe the setting. State what you hope the audience will know or do as a result of hearing your talk or reading your document. Don't apologize in advance or introduce too many contingencies, but try to set the scene so the volunteer critic can play his or her role fully.

You might ask your reader to make an outline of the document or talk or a list of its main points as that person perceives them. This will help you determine if what you intended to say comes through to the reader. Be sure, too, to indicate the level of verification you desire: Should the reader focus just on effectiveness? Or just on conventionality? Or look at everything? And make clear that the final responsibility for the work is yours. You want a helper, not a coconspirator.

Helping Others to Verify Their Communication Product

If you ask others to help verify your work, be prepared to do the same for them. Be a willing editor when called on to cast a critical eye at someone else's draft letter. Sit through a rehearsal of some friends' presentation and give them your best ideas for improvement. (See Chapters 10 and 11 for additional advice on collaborative editing.)

Learning occurs through feedback. The more good feedback you get, the more you learn. When you give feedback, try to learn from it yourself. Start with what's good, what works. Say, specifically, why. Then note points for improvement, again being specific. No one is helped by a sweeping comment such as, "It's great. Don't change a thing." Similarly, it isn't useful to say, "I just don't like it." Give details, point to specifics, make concrete suggestions for changes.

Whether you're on the giving or receiving end of feedback, as an editor or someone whose work is being verified by others, you can improve your own skills by paying attention to effectiveness, efficiency, and conventions. The work you do should meet your expectations, follow your outline, and achieve its purpose for the intended audience. Even when someone helps you, it's your job to verify that the communication product does all that.

SCENARIO

Getting and Giving Help in Editing

Because of declining worldwide telecommunications demand, top management of a multinational corporation producing chips for wireless telephones decided to idle two plants, one in Ireland and one in the United States, and consolidate production at its Taiwan facility. Taiwan would have to produce more than it had before, but by doing so at a single facility the company hoped to achieve gains in asset use and therefore profitability.

It fell to Wang Lee, operations manager of the Taiwan plant, to develop a plan to accomplish the new goals. He was to submit a brief written report to senior management and then to appear at the company's headquarters in Sweden to present his recommendations orally and answer questions. The basic strategy was clear to Lee: move to 24/7 production—that is, work around the clock. But whether to accomplish that through adding a third eight-hour shift or by moving to two twelve-hour shifts puzzled him. Adding a whole new shift would be more expensive; the incremental cost of stretching the current two eight-hour shifts into twelve-hour shifts would be less so. But workers at the plant would not be happy about the change, and quality control, a high priority, could suffer if workers took on such long hours.

Lee worked through the issues and concluded that he would recommend two twelve-hour shifts, notwithstanding his unease about worker response and the possible impact on quality. He drafted a seven-page report that began with the need to go with a 24/7 operation and then evaluated alternatives, listing strengths and weaknesses of each and emphasizing the financial impact. The report ended with a simple conclusion: "I therefore recommend that we adopt two twelve-hour production shifts, effective immediately."

A native Chinese speaker, Lee also spoke and wrote English well because of his graduate school experience in the U.K. and a two-year assignment at the company's Texas facility. Although based in Sweden, the company used English as its official language, and Lee was always nervous about whether his command of the language was adequate. Career advancement required fluent English.

Lee decided to seek help on his draft report. Hugh McPherson, a Scot who served as the financial director of the Taiwan plant, was an old friend from graduate school days. Angela Larson, an American now based in Sweden, was on temporary assignment in Taiwan to review the plant's human resource function. Because both spoke English as a first language and each had expertise in issues important in the proposed change—finances and employee relations—Lee was confident they could help him improve the written report and coach him on the oral presentation he would make at headquarters.

"Please correct my English," Lee told Hugh and Angela over tea in his office. "I want to do the best job on this." They agreed to review Wang's draft and give him their comments early the next morning.

Aside from a few spelling errors and some rigidly formal language, Angela found the report's writing to be clear. But she felt it spent too much time in the opening section about the need to adopt a 24/7 schedule, an obvious point that she thought Lee belabored at the expense of digging deeper into the alternatives. When she talked to Hugh before going back to see Lee, he agreed that the language was not a problem. "The problem," he told Angela, "is the conclusion." Lee presents good arguments for going to three shifts, and points out the quality problem in the two-shift approach, but then he ends by saying 'go to two.' I don't think his heart's in that conclusion. He just throws it in at the end, without support."

Angela and Hugh decided to consolidate their suggestions and produced an outline of a new version of the report that would address the weaknesses they saw in its structure and argument. When they presented it to Lee, he thanked them politely and asked if they had edited the report.

They then produced their copies, with errors corrected and suggestions on words and phrasing. "Thank you very much, indeed," Lee said. "You will make me into a good writer of English yet!" As they left his office, Angela and Hugh noticed that Lee pushed their suggested outline to the edge of his desk as he sat down in front of his computer with their editing suggestions in front of him and a look of determination on his face.

Questions for Discussion

1. At which level of verification—effectiveness, efficiency, conventionality—did Lee want his colleagues to help him?
2. At which level did they respond?
3. Did Lee make clear in his instructions what help he wanted? How might he have clarified or enhanced those instructions?
4. What should Angela and Hugh have done when Lee first invited them to help? How might they have refined his instructions at the beginning?
5. Are Angela and Hugh's suggestions helpful? How could they have been more helpful?

PART
II
Communicating in Groups

CHAPTER 10 Managing Group Communication

Because business is conducted in and through groups, experienced managers know a great deal about group dynamics, from both formal education and practical experience. To draw out that knowledge, this chapter briefly reviews general characteristics of group process. It then presents the 4-S approach to communicating in groups and offers guidelines for managing team writing and speaking projects.

Understanding Group Dynamics and Team Process

Whatever their goals, all groups have to get started and then do their work. How they form and how they function directly influence their outcomes.

How Groups Form

Groups either form themselves or are formed by someone outside them, usually a person occupying a higher organizational position than anyone in the group. The difference carries important implications for how groups function.

A self-formed group knows its mission; it forms precisely to resolve a problem or produce a product. If, for example, the staff of the marketing department of an insurance company needs a brochure to describe a new product, several persons might group themselves to produce it. As it begins, the self-formed group has to discuss explicitly the features of its work. It must determine the outcome (the final communication product) and the processes for achieving it: setting schedules, selecting a leader, assigning tasks.

When a group is formed by someone outside it, that person should make all the elements of the assignment explicit. The product is defined, the deadline set, questions about audience and outcome settled. An appointed group also usually has an appointed leader. An appointed group has obvious advantages in this regard because it doesn't need to take time to select a leader and decide on outcomes and schedules: it can get right to work on the central issue. But an executive appointing a group has to be clear in providing instructions. She can't say, "Put together something on this new product." Instead, she has to say, "I want a two-fold brochure in three colors that our sales staff can use to describe the new annuity product, and I need it ready for production by the end of the month at the latest." For an appointed group, the difference between a general assignment and a specific one is often the difference between failure and success: the tighter the instructions, the better the outcome.

How Groups Work

Although every group, however formed, establishes and follows processes unique to it, there are general patterns in group development and behavior. Particularly important are listening, negotiation and conflict management, and exploiting group diversity.

Stages of Group Work Groups move through stages that are commonly called forming, storming, norming, performing, and adjourning. We've just discussed *forming*. *Storming* refers to the period when members of the group debate and discuss objectives, processes, leadership, deadlines. In this stage, the storm metaphor may be misunderstood to imply the angry hurling of thunderbolts; instead, it simply refers to an unsettled atmosphere as the group moves toward resolution of preliminary issues. This resolution comes in the *norming* stage, when the group establishes its rules of operation, or norms of behavior. Members then turn to the work itself—*performing*. When the work is done, the group has reached the *adjourning* stage. As you'll see, the 4-S model for managing group communication conforms to this forming-storming-norming-performing-adjourning pattern.

Styles of Group Behavior Three styles of group behavior are common: conflict, conformity, and consensus. *Conflict* occurs naturally as different points of view are presented, discussed, and debated. *Conformity* is a typical response to conflict and occurs when people decide they want to move on. The danger of conformity is that members of a group may tend to accept bad ideas—or at least ideas they don't really agree with—either

Focus

- on the *speaker:* establish eye contact, be aware of body language, pay attention to emphasis—that is, on what the speaker seems to think is important in what she is saying.
- on the *message:* listen for key ideas and major issues rather than details.
- on the *situation:* devote your attention to what's being said by whom, and don't be distracted by irrelevant issues or by the circumstances of the meeting.

Restrain

- your *emotions:* avoid making judgments about what is being said and who is saying it.
- your *impatience:* let the speaker finish, don't interrupt, and don't try to finish the speaker's thoughts.

Adopt

- the *speaker's point of view:* try to imagine being the speaker, following his order of presentation and analysis rather than imposing your own.
- a *group perspective:* try to imagine your group as a single person, in which individual ideas function as if they were spoken by the same person rather than by some "other."

Figure 10.1 | Listening Skills

because the ideas are presented by others with greater authority or because members of the group simply don't want to spend time on a contentious issue. Overemphasis on conformity leads to "groupthink," which produces automatic responses, unexamined assumptions, and tired ideas.

The most effective group behavior is *consensus,* which occurs when members truly agree. Reaching consensus requires open discussion—and open minds. Members of the group must be willing to listen as well as to speak and need common objectives and an agreed-on process to resolve conflict.

Listening in Groups Good listening skills promote successful collaboration. Good listeners *focus, restrain,* and *adopt.* See Figure 10.1.

Negotiation and Conflict Management Conflicts are expected and desirable in groups. They reflect the richness and complexity that provide the very reason for working in groups—to bring forth different ideas, information, and perspectives that result from varying experiences and talents. Conflicts can't be wished away. Instead, they need to be managed so the group moves toward consensus. Conflict management is a form of negotiation. The following negotiation techniques help in managing conflicts that arise in groups:

- *Focus on ideas and information, not personalities.* Emotional responses to individuals impede conflict management. Try to identify the source of the conflict in the *content* of the message rather than its communicator.
- *Agree on what you agree on.* Find common ground, and narrow areas of disagreement to specific ideas that can be addressed in the context of larger areas of agreement. Identify clearly the source of disagreement so you can focus on resolving it and not waste time discussing what you already agree on. Common ground provides a place where *mutual* gains can be achieved.
- *Deal with what matters.* Weigh the significance of an area of disagreement and calibrate the energy and emotion of dealing with it to its importance. Don't get hung up on details or waste time over small points.
- *Discuss tradeoffs openly.* Don't pretend that "everyone wins" when major disagreements need to be resolved. Specify what is being given up and what is being gained as the group moves toward consensus.
- *Accept what you can't change.* You can't use negotiation to change basic personalities or make people into something they're not. Accept differences.
- *Use objective criteria.* State problems so that you can use measurable standards. If you define success as "being the best," you increase the likelihood of disagreements. Instead, use an objective standard (e.g., "50 percent of the aggregate market") that can be the basis of rational discussion and ultimate resolution. Quibbling over qualitative words can engender unnecessary disagreement.
- *Move on.* Once a consensus has been reached, don't keep wrestling with the issue, raise it for further consideration, or try to modify the outcome.

Perhaps the biggest problem in managing conflict in groups is the tendency to ignore it. Like anxiety, conflict grows if it's ignored. Group members need to admit the conflict, see it as a natural outgrowth of differing perspectives and experiences, and then focus on working toward consensus. Pretending conflict doesn't exist only deepens the conflict and impedes efforts to manage it.

Exploiting Group Diversity Although group conflict can arise from group diversity, group success is also often a product of that diversity. Getting diverse viewpoints that come out of different experiences and backgrounds is, after all, one of the best reasons to work in groups.

Diversity results from differences in position and responsibility, personalities, learning styles, experiences, expectations, culture, age, race, and gender. In general, the greater the diversity, the wider will be the range of viewpoints and expertise available to solve the problem. At the same time, the greater the diversity, the harder the group will have to work in listening and managing potential conflict. For example, a group of ten persons may include three high-level executives and seven junior staff members; two may be Asian, two Hispanic, four American, and two French; six may be women and four men; two may have deep experience with the specific problem the group is addressing, whereas eight may be relatively new to it. A heterogeneous group such as this may appear to present problems in coordination and leadership, consensus building, and smooth operation, but it is also more likely to produce a solid outcome that derives from multiple viewpoints and addresses issues no individual may see or understand. While a more homogeneous group may appear to ease some of the process problems of a heterogeneous one, it is also less likely to succeed—less likely to produce a final work product that addresses all issues effectively.

Using the 4-S Model to Create a Team Product

To create a communication product—a written proposal, a sales presentation, an instructional video—a team should follow the **4-S** model:

- *Scope* the work.
- *Schedule* the work.
- *Stay* in touch.
- *Satisfy* all needs.

Scope the Work

The group's first job is to scope the work by discussing the *product,* the *people,* and the *process.*

Product Clearly identify the product the group will create. Review the situation to answer the four questions of the analysis phase of the management communication process (see Chapters 3 and 4): what? to whom? how? when? Some or all of the questions will be answered by the group's initial assignment. For example, if the group has been formed to produce a ten-minute video introducing new employees to the company's performance evaluation process, the *whom* and *how* issues are explicitly answered (it's a video for new employees). The *what* and *when* may be explicitly answered in the group's assignment. However, they may often be only implicit and therefore in need of fleshing out, probably by going back to the person who formed the group to get clear directions on the outcome desired from the audience and the date when the video is due.

The tangible outcome of this phase of scoping is a *product plan*—a detailed outline of the final product, a schematic of what the document or talk will include and in what order. The outline (see Chapter 6) serves as a routine reminder to group members of the overall project and the outcome. At the end, when the work is done, the outline provides a means to verify whether the product meets the identified goals.

Clarifying the intended communication product—making sure everyone in the group knows the goal and outlining the outcome in a product plan—is so important and so obvious that groups sometimes move from that step to others without considering two equally important aspects of the preliminary scoping work. A group needs to give serious attention to the people who will do the work and the process they will follow.

People Who's in the group? What do they know and what can they do? Are skills needed beyond those represented by members? Should the group ask to augment its numbers? Or does it have too many of one kind of expert? Address questions like these openly when the group first meets. Assessing the talent pool candidly will help the group spot holes that need to be filled and will make assignment of duties easier. There is never a perfect group, but if some critical skills are obviously missing, it's the group's responsibility to remedy the problem.

Process Groups that bog down in process risk never creating a product, but groups that neglect process rarely create the best product they are capable of. The amount and type of attention that process deserves in group communication depend on the size and nature of the group, the complexity of the project, and the schedule on which the group is working. A group of three or four persons who have worked together often and successfully and are assigned a relatively simple project to be completed in a few days need not linger long over process. On the other hand, a large group—and especially one composed of people who haven't worked together much—that faces a large project with a long time horizon needs to devote considerable attention to process up front.

The chief process issues to be addressed are the mode of operation, the mode of communication, and leadership.

Mode of Operation Will the group work informally, or will there be formal lines of authority? Will decisions be made consensually or according to expertise or organizational authority? Will tasks be divided according to the issues inherent in the project (accountants work on financial projections, market analysts work on promotional schemes, engineers focus on production, and so on)? Or will the division of labor reflect the communication product (one person to write the introduction and conclusion, two to develop the body of the report, a third to serve as editor)? Resolve such issues at the outset to smooth the work itself.

Mode of Communication Even as the group works on a communication product for its assigned audience, it will produce many communication products among group members along the way: memos and e-mails back and forth between team members, drafts of text for review, questions about what to include and exclude, visuals to be reviewed collectively for their effectiveness. Each of these intragroup communications follows the basic communication model (see Chapter 1). But the group needs to decide on the approach (formal vs. informal) and the communication networks to follow (for example, a wheel network in which all information is funneled to one person, or a chain in which messages are conveyed along a prescribed route).

Leadership Except in a very small and informal group where the members work together smoothly according to long practice, any group requires explicit leadership. Someone has to be in charge. Someone has to remind members of their responsibilities, check on progress, convene meetings as needed, and take the lead in bringing the project to its conclusion.

That leader may be designated by the person appointing the group, or she may be selected by the group at its first meeting based on her experience and expertise. It's rare to select a group leader by formal balloting, but it's important that everyone leave the first meeting knowing who the leader is. Don't assume Juanita is the group leader just because she's the senior member of the staff. Make sure the leadership decision is explicit and fully understood.

In large groups facing complex tasks, it's helpful to identify several leaders, each one to coordinate a different task: an overall coordinator who makes sure everything's running smoothly and takes final authority for bringing the project to a successful conclusion, a second person to serve as editor, and a third person to handle process issues like scheduling meetings and the flow of documents. The extent to which these duties can be combined in one person or distributed among several depends on the project and the team.

In a large group working on a complex project over an extended period, process issues like operation, communication, and leadership are appropriately summarized in a "charter," a brief, written record of how the group has agreed to work. Even in a small group, or one working on a small project on a short deadline, an informal charter is advisable. It can take the form of a summary statement by the team leader: "We've agreed to . . ." Making explicit, in written or oral form, the rules of the road will help to surface disagreement or confusion early on, when they can be productively addressed, and will ease the work itself by clarifying how it will get done.

Schedule the Work

When a group finishes scoping its work, it should know the tasks to be done and have a good sense of who in the group will do what. It should also have a clear understanding of the overall schedule—when the final (and, before that, a draft) product is due, and when subordinate parts will be complete or ready for group review.

Bring these items together in a workplan that assigns tasks to individual group members and puts due dates on each. If possible, build in some slack time—at least a few days between the group's completion and the due date for the product—to accommodate changes that happen along the way and to make revisions before the final product is submitted.

The workplan can range from a simple chart to an elaborate critical path method (CPM) display. The nature of the work and the time assigned for it determine the formality and detail of the plan. Figure 10.2 presents a simple workplan for the project described in this chapter's Scenario.

Most important is that the group create—and agree to—the workplan as early as possible in the collaborative process. Ideally, the group should create the plan at the end of its first meeting and then circulate it among members for further comments. If the scoping work takes the entire

WHAT?	WHO?	WHEN?
Draft core message	Tanya	12/29; 3:00 P.M. e-mail
Review and revise core message	Tanya, Mitch, Hugh	12/29; 4:00 P.M. call
Approve core message	Ellen, Max	12/29; before 6:00 P.M. call
Talk with senior managers	Ellen, Max	12/30
Draft media and employee meeting announcements	Tanya	Ready for 12/30–31 meeting
Draft employee statements	Mitch, Hugh	Ready for 12/30–31 meeting
Draft media announcement, Q&A	Tanya	Ready for 12/30–31 meeting
Draft shareholder letters	Mitch, Tanya	Ready for 12/30–31 meeting
Review and approve all drafts	Mitch, Tanya, Hugh	At 12/30–31 meeting, Baltimore
Approve all drafts	Ellen, Max	by 1/1
Send announcement of employee meetings	Mitch, Hugh	1/2
Send announcement of media conferences	Tanya	1/2
Mail shareholder letters	Mitch, Tanya	1/2
Employee and media conferences	Ellen, Max, Tanya, Mitch	1/3

Figure 10.2 Simple Workplan for Crisis Communication (Based on the scenario on pp. 163–167)

first meeting, reconvene for a second meeting for the single purpose of distilling assignments into a schedule.

When the workplan is ready, all members should review it and sign off. Buy-in is essential because the schedule drives the work. Obviously, circumstances will change as the work progresses, especially if the project is large and spread over a considerable time span. The schedule may need to change, too, with appropriate agreement along the way. But even though it's subject to revision, the schedule of assignments and dates has to be in place at the outset.

Stay in Touch

Guided by the product plan and the workplan, group members set about their work. But they also need to stay in touch, formally and informally. The group leader (or the persons specifically designated to watch over the process) has to see to that. Once assigned a task, most people like to get to work on it and regard checking back in with someone as a distraction. It can be, but failure to keep in regular contact as the pieces of a project are being worked on can create severe problems. It's easy to lose sight of the overall objectives if you're working on one piece, but checking back in reminds you of where you're headed—and the role your part of the project plays in getting there.

As the work proceeds, one person has to keep asking questions of the others, questions about both the process and the product, questions that will reveal potential problems in timing or content, questions that will keep the work in focus for all members.

Satisfy All Needs

When the work is complete, check it against the original analysis and the product plan to be sure it satisfies all the needs the group identified during its scoping work. Does the communication product do what it's supposed to for the intended audience in the right form and on time? If not, the group should be able to identify deficiencies and remedy them. (That's one of the reasons you always try to build slack time into a schedule.)

If the product is fully verifiable against the analysis and product plan, the group's work is *almost* done. Satisfying substantive needs—verifying that the communication product is right—is obviously critical. But even when that product is complete, don't ignore the process that produced it. Individuals learn to be effective team members by working on effective teams, and making explicit the nature of the group processes improves the chances for individual and group learning. So when the work is complete, celebrate—and then discuss the process itself: What worked and what didn't? How can strong features of the process be carried into other group situations? How can weak ones be avoided in the future? What individual member's skills need to be refined or augmented? The group should ask what it can learn from its experience.

Managing Team Writing Projects

When you are a member of a team whose outcome is a document like a proposal or report, you need to address issues unique to writing projects. You need to determine who will do the writing and how to achieve a unified verbal effect.

Who Writes?

How does a group produce a single written document? You can follow one of three models:

- Cowriting
- Single writer
- Multiple writers, single editor

Each has advantages and disadvantages, and the choice of approach depends on the nature of the group and the nature of the project—its length, scope, size, and complexity. Within one project, all three approaches might be used at different points. To select wisely, you need to understand each model.

Cowriting When all or most members of a group actually write all or parts of the document, the process is called cowriting. Two or more people sit before a computer or pad of paper and draft prose, discussing organization, forming sentences and paragraphs, making word choices. Cowriting employs circle or all-channel networks of organizational communication as messages pass back and forth among interested groups (circles) or all members of the group (all-channel).

Cowriting is demanding and works best for small segments of writing that present special problems. For example, several people might jointly thrash out an introduction or a conclusion, testing tone and language selection as they go along. Segments of a written document that have been developed by individual members of the group lend themselves less well to cowriting since individual experts have the best sense of content.

Single Writer Groups sometimes decide that one member has special writing skills. ("You were an English major, John; you should write this up.") If so, there's an obvious advantage to having that person do the actual writing. This approach requires team members to feed material to the designated writer as they produce drafts to avoid sinking him or her under the weight of all the drafts just before the final version is due. A single writer can then shape organization and language incrementally rather than facing a pile of paper at the end, when changes are harder to make. Even when the single writer model is used, group members must be aware that they are actually producing text themselves as they go along rather than dictating notes for the writer to make sense of.

Multiple Writers, Single Editor In practice, many groups use the multiple writers, single editor approach because it captures some of the qualities of both the cowriting and single writer approaches. This approach uses the chain and wheel forms of organizational communication. In the chain, versions of text are passed along to other members for review and revision, ending up with the single editor who pulls it together. In the wheel network, the editor sits at the center and receives and sends material (drafts) back and forth to others who are writing them. In either model, the editor and writers must be in regular contact. The editor should not be thought of as the person who comes in at the end of the process to wave a magic linguistic wand over the various bits of text to produce a polished final version. He or she must work sequentially through the process, advising writers as they produce drafts, making suggestions, carrying ideas from one person to another.

One Voice

Regardless of how many hands, or fingers, were involved in producing a group document, it should have one voice. It should read as if written by one person. It should have a distinctive *brand.*

In *content,* that means that no part should contradict or call into question another part. The introductory and concluding sections should be consistent, and evidence presented in the middle should support both.

In *style,* that means maintaining a single tone, using a consistent level of language (formal or informal, technical or popular) throughout, and maintaining conventions (for example, if you use references, be sure you use them throughout and don't allow footnotes to creep in because one member of the team used them).

To test if a group document has one voice, ask someone or several people outside the group to read it. Tell the reader that it's a group document and ask for suggestions to improve its consistency in content and style. Just as it's hard to be a good editor of your own prose, so a group is challenged to read its work with detachment. (For more on editing, see Chapter 9.)

Managing Team Speaking Projects

When the outcome of a team project is an oral presentation, the group has to address the question of who speaks. The group also needs to pay particular attention to logistics and practice the presentation in a run-through.

Who Speaks?

The first issue facing a team working on an oral communication product is "Who speaks?" There are two basic models:

- Single presenter
- Multiple presenters

The nature of the project, the size of the team, and the circumstances of the presentation—place, audience, time—determine which model is best.

Single Presenter Even though a group may have done all the work on the project, one member may present the results. A single presenter simplifies matters. She can control the tone and pace, keep the audience focused on the content in the way the group wants, and speak with one clear voice. If one person does the presentation, she will of course acknowledge at the outset the group who did the work, and since it's desirable for the group to be present she should introduce them. In the single-presenter model, it's also typical for members of the group to answer questions at the end on matters for which they had responsibility.

A single presenter may be the group leader or the person who served as editor and coordinator. But it may also be a member of the group who is experienced at speaking and conveys a professional attitude when he stands in front of a crowd. Whatever role the presenter played in the work itself, he needs to become intimately familiar with the topic to speak with authority. At the run-through (see below), the presenter should seek and follow advice from others in the group on what to say and how to say it.

Multiple Presenters Having all or at least more than one member of the group do the presentation offers advantages and some challenges. When the people who did the work present it, their participation lends authority to the talk and gives individual experts the chance to elaborate on their areas of interest. Multiple presenters also convey something about the nature of the work—the seriousness with which it was performed, the many people involved in it, the significance of the audience gathered to hear the results.

But having more than one speaker risks distractions. Good logistics and an effective run-through help overcome that potential problem, but there's no way to avoid completely a lack of smoothness and clarity of focus when different speakers come and go during the presentation. The audience may dwell on the second speaker's points while the third is beginning, or it may find the clothes or presentational style of one speaker coloring what another says and does.

To minimize distractions and retain maximum focus for the audience with multiple speakers, it is essential to have a leader, a master of ceremonies. That person

- welcomes the audience.
- introduces the other speakers.
- provides an overview of the presentation.
- choreographs the coming and going of speakers.
- takes questions and directs them to group members for answers.
- concludes the presentation with thanks and any appropriate words about the next step.

The master of ceremonies or team leader has to simultaneously keep an eye on the clock, on the audience, and on the speakers. His job is to be the point person and run the show. Because he concentrates on the process of the presentation, the lead presenter should not have a substantive role in the presentation—that is, he should not present content areas. Introductions and conclusions may, or may not, be within his sphere. But he has his hands full getting the show on the road and moving it smoothly to a successful conclusion.

Logistics

In addition to the logistical issues common to any presentation (see Chapter 7), group presentations raise the special problem of choreography—of managing the appearances of multiple speakers. Think of your group presentation as a stage performance—a play or dance. Just as you expect dancers to move in the same direction and actors to enter at the right time to exchange dialogue, so your audience expects an orderly flow of presenters. The audience perceives badly choreographed presentations as confused—possibly even chaotic—and that obviously undermines the content of the presentation and credibility of the team.

To avoid the appearance of confusion, the group needs to choreograph its movements, beginning with the initial view the audience has of the group and extending through to the last, when the group leaves the room. Led by whichever member serves as team leader or master of ceremonies, the group needs to address these questions:

- *How to start?* Will the group be assembled before the audience arrives, or will members enter afterward? If your group presentation is one of several that the audience will hear, each group will probably be ushered in after the last is ushered out. This is often the case in sales presentations when several groups are scheduled to make their pitches in succession. It's important in this circumstance that the group follow instructions and take positions promptly, without lingering for side-bar conversations among members. A crisp, professional attitude is reflected in a quick, orderly entrance.
- *Where to sit—or stand?* Will the group sit or stand? Will all members be assembled at a table facing the audience? Or will each member sit in a chair and move to a podium to speak as his or her turn arises? If one person is speaking for the group, will the other members be seated beside or in front, ready to answer questions or provide elaboration on points? Be sure you know the seating or standing arrangements and plan accordingly.
- *How to hand off?* In a presentation where several persons speak, handing off needs to be as smooth as the passing of the baton in a relay. When one finishes speaking, she should then identify who is

next and quickly move away (if each speaker speaks at a single podium) or turn to look at the next speaker (if all are seated at one table) as a sign that it's that person's turn. Practice smooth passes.

- *How to end?* A ragged ending can undermine otherwise strong group presentations. The group member who closes the presentation should leave a single, strong impression. The group's leaving should reinforce that impression. Hanging around to pick up slides or converse internally while the audience sits uncomfortably reduces the impact of a tight and well delivered presentation. Avoid ragged endings and the sense that the group doesn't know how to conduct itself once the presentation is over.

Run-Through

Choreography is part of the preparation for an effective group presentation and is best tested in the run-through. Always practice. In a group presentation, the run-through is perhaps even more important than in an individual presentation because each member of the group represents an independent variable.

You practice not just the words of the delivery but the play itself. In a play, actors practice their lines individually, but they then assemble to rehearse the whole play. The run-through is a chance to sharpen the choreography as well as the individual talks. It helps you spot potential problems in using equipment, dimming lights, handing off from one speaker to the next. It gives you the chance to see—and debug—the whole presentation in addition to the individual parts. And it's the whole presentation that creates the brand—the strong, clear impression that reinforces the message.

SCENARIO

A Team Takes on a Communication Challenge

When the phone conversation with Ellen Polster ended, Mitch Owens knew that the ski vacation he had planned for New Year's weekend wasn't going to happen. Polster, CEO of Great Lakes Airlines (GLA), had warned Mitch that the merger was getting close, but he had still hoped it wouldn't happen until after the holiday. Her call at noon on Wednesday, December 29, confirmed that the boards of GLA and AirEast had just approved the merger, subject to the vote of the shareholders of both companies. As vice president for corporate affairs at GLA, Mitch was responsible for public relations, investor relations, and human resources—three areas immediately affected by the merger, because communication with the media, shareholders, and employees was essential. "Sorry about your ski trip, Mitch," Ellen said at the end of the call. "It looks like a long work weekend for all of us. We'll have a conference call at 3:00 P.M. to discuss strategy."

The strategy Ellen referred to concerned the timing and content of announcements about the merger. Mitch joined Ellen in her office for the call. From AirEast, the participants were

- Max Denton, CEO
- Tanya Templeton, director of public and investor relations
- Hugh Santoro, director of human resources.

"I'm hoping Tanya, Hugh, and Mitch can handle this," Max said after the introductions and congratulations about the deal. "Ellen and I are exhausted from putting this together."

Mitch noticed Ellen frown before she responded. "Speak for yourself, Max," she said. "Announcing this is as important as doing the deal in the first place, so we've got to get it right."

"I agree with that, Ellen," Max responded, "but I think we can trust our folks to handle the details once we agree on the parameters. And I'd like to see Tanya lead this since she's got experience in crisis communication. You remember that minor accident AirEast had two years ago? Tanya coordinated our operations on that."

Ellen glanced at Mitch, who nodded in agreement. The five participants, led by Tanya, agreed on a schedule in which no public announcements would be made until Monday, January 3, at the end of the New Year's holiday weekend. Before then,

- Each CEO would notify senior managers in person and confidentially, beginning immediately after the conference call.
- Starting Thursday, January 30, the two CEOs would phone or visit key local, state, and federal officials on whose goodwill the approval of the deal would hinge and who would not want to be blind-sided by an unexpected public announcement. While the

long holiday weekend might make it hard to reach these individuals, a positive consequence was that it was also a time when the news was unlikely to be leaked to the media.

- On Sunday, January 2, releases would be sent to announce two media conferences on Monday, one in Baltimore, AirEast's home, and one in Minneapolis, GLA's. Also on Sunday, notices would go out by e-mail and physical notices would be posted at all job sites to call employee meetings for 9:00 A.M., Monday, January 3.
- A letter from each CEO to shareholders would be mailed Sunday. Although they would learn of the merger through Monday's formal announcement at the media conferences, shareholders would get their own letter on Tuesday or Wednesday.

With the schedule agreed to, the participants in the conference call decided to leave the drafting of releases and letters to Mitch, Tanya, and Hugh. All five would have another conference call at 6:00 P.M. to review progress. Mitch left Ellen's office for his own to call Tanya and Hugh so they could begin developing the messages. Although he was responsible for public relations, Mitch viewed himself as more of a general manager than a media specialist and was glad that Tanya had experience in crisis communication.

"The first thing we need to do," Tanya said when the three were connected by phone, "is to shape the core message—the key idea we want to put out there."

"But it's really a couple of messages, isn't it?" Mitch asked. "We have to communicate with the public, shareholders, and our employees, and they all have different interests."

"True," Tanya said, "but the core has to be the same. We can't be saying one thing to one group and something different to others. We have to shade the message for each audience, but the core is the same. Let's see if we can put together a paragraph that says it all. I'll be happy to take a shot at that and get it to you two by e-mail by 3:00. Then we can conference again at 4:00 and see where we are." Mitch said he was happy to have Tanya do the writing.

"Any special angles we need to cover out there?" she asked.

"Two that I can think of right away," he answered. "The first is that Minneapolis went to bat for us with the state two years ago to get some special tax breaks. And the second is our employees—we're not employee-owned or anything like that, but Ellen has always worked very well with our employees to keep them happy—and non-union! Unlike most airlines, we have great labor relations, and we need to keep them that way."

"Lucky you," Hugh said. "I've got four unions to deal with here."

"How's it going to work after the merger?" Mitch asked.

"Not something we can deal with now, Mitch," Tanya said. "But I'll try to shape the message to emphasize your good-citizen image and your happy workers. Anything else?"

Mitch couldn't think of additional sensitive issues but was concerned about the confidentiality of e-mail. Tanya and Hugh agreed but concluded there was no better alternative, given the need for quick turnaround.

"Faxes can go astray just as easily," Tanya said, and so they decided to proceed with e-mail, sending and receiving only among the three of them, since they knew the CEOs delegated e-mail reading to secretaries. "I'll also sketch out a workplan for us," Tanya added. "A to-do list with names and dates, just to capture what we've agreed to." (See Figure 10.2.)

Just before 3:00, Tanya's e-mail came through:

AirEast and Great Lakes Airlines are merging to form Northern Airways. The new company will be the ninth-largest airline carrier in the United States, serving 28 cities in the Northeast and Midwest. Key benefits of the merger include enhanced financial strength, increased competitive capacity, and better service for flyers.

That's it? Mitch replied as soon as he read it.

It's the core message, Mitch, Tanya responded. *Of course we need to flesh out details for the different target groups, but what I'm trying to catch here is the essence. Anything to add to that?*

Mitch, sensitive to employee concerns at GLA, suggested something be added on that issue.

It's implicit in the financial strength and competitive capacity points, Tanya responded, *but if Hugh doesn't see any union problems I can make it explicit. How about if I add "a stronger airline that offers a stable working environment for employees"?*

Might be a problem, Hugh said in his first e-mail response to the core message. *The unions could see that as a red flag, or maybe even an opening for bargaining for higher wages. Can't we just say something about the new airline being a good place to work?*

Mitch agreed, and Tanya modified the statement and sent the new version to both of them just before their scheduled 4:00 P.M. conference call.

At the start of the call, they agreed on the new message and also agreed to review a physical copy of it with their CEOs before the 6:00 general conference call.

"Now comes the fun stuff," Tanya said. "Assuming Max and Ellen sign off, we have to start getting the other documents ready. We need a release to announce the media conferences on Monday, the employee announcement of their meetings, then formal statements to be ready at both the media and employee conferences, a Q&A list, and of course the shareholder letters."

"Sounds right to me," Mitch said.

"Agree," Hugh added.

Tanya suggested that Mitch fly to Baltimore so the group could go over all the materials in person.

Mitch agreed, saying he would review the core message with Ellen, check schedules to see how soon he could get to Baltimore, and get back to them with details.

"Looks okay to me," Ellen said of the message. "We'll need a lot more details, but I agree that's the message we want to send. What do you think the issues are going to be, especially the conflicts, the tough stuff?"

Mitch listed them:

- the need to shade the messages differently for the two employee groups since one was unionized and one wasn't.
- the timing of Monday's employee and media meetings, given the one-hour time difference between Baltimore and Minneapolis.
- the challenge in keeping the focus positive despite the uncertainties that a merger brings.
- the loss of identity for both companies when they assumed a new name.
- the questions about control and jobs in the new company.

"Sounds like you've got a good handle on all this, Mitch," Ellen said after he had explained the points. "Don't hesitate to call me any time while you've over there working with them. I'll be happy to run interference with Max if you can't resolve them among yourselves."

Questions for Discussion

1. How was this group formed? Does that method lead to any potential problems in how it does its work? Would a different means of group formation be possible—and desirable?
2. Are the group's instructions clear?
3. Does the group create a "charter" to guide its work?
4. How effective is its workplan? Should it also have product plans?
5. Which mode of production (single writer, multiple writers, multiple writers/single editor) does the group seem to be following? What are the strengths and weaknesses of that approach? Would you recommend a different mode?
6. Do personal ambitions or "politics" play a role in the way the group behaves?
7. What are the advantages and disadvantages of the group's working electronically instead of face to face?
8. Is it clear what the group needs to do next? And *how* it will do it?

CHAPTER

Collaborating with Technology

Information technology allows individuals at a distance from one another in geography or time to collaborate on communication products. This chapter applies the advice on communicating in teams you read about in Chapter 10 to a predominantly virtual environment. It discusses strategies for using the tools of a digital workspace to conduct meetings, stay in touch, annotate drafts of a communication product, and capture knowledge of the team's processes and products. A virtual environment adds a new dimension to the team's work that provides both challenges and enhancements.

Developing the Virtual Team

Cross-cultural, cross-functional teams that work remotely offer many advantages, especially the ability to bring a diversity of expertise and local experience to business opportunities across the globe. Such teams form and disband as opportunities dictate. Information technology enables their work—and allows them to work rapidly to take advantage of new opportunities in the marketplace.

Selecting the Appropriate Technology

The first task the team faces is selecting the appropriate technology. That decision depends, in part, on the technology currently used by team members, the number of people on the team, their familiarity with each other, their location relative to each other, and the priority and time frame of the collaborative product. In general, choose the simplest technology that can get the job done (Figure 11.1).

TOOL	ADVANTAGES	DISADVANTAGES
Telephone	Everywhere, especially wireless cell phones As voice mail, easily crosses time and work zones Familiar, no real learning curve to operate Relatively inexpensive	Voice only
E-mail	Widely available Easy to send and receive Accommodates attached documents Available for PCs, PDAs, cell phones Instant messaging, Listservs, and chat rooms	Systems may go down Only cryptic messages for PDAs and cell phones Requires equipment and network link Higher investment than phone
Web-based workspace	Integration of text, voice, video, data Incorporates several applications to foster group work on documents Greater security than e-mail	Higher investment than phone May require training to use More subject to breakdown than phone
Dedicated videoconference room	Multichannel media, with large panel display to integrate video, sound, visuals, text among sites Simulates face-to-face meeting with kinesic cues	Most expensive and restrictive All sites need similar equipment

Figure 11.1 | Electronic Tools for the Virtual Team

Team member ____________________

Site ____________________

Technology available (e.g., personal computers with Internet and e-mail access? Telephones for conference calls? Dedicated videoconference room?)

Support available (e.g., technician on site? Support only on certain days? No support?)

Training needed

Figure 11.2 | Checklist: Current Status of Technology for Team Support

Assessing Current Technology Use As a baseline for that selection, each team member should complete a technology status report (Figure 11.2). The team leader then compiles the reports to determine what technology is shared and how experienced and comfortable team members are with collaborative technology.

Accommodating the Team's Work Consider, too, the team's logistics and goals. For example, a team of seven persons, each at a different location but each with good Internet access, who are working on a series of high-priority documents concerning a corporate merger, may want to rent a secure digital workspace on the Web where they can share and comment on documents easily and rapidly. A team of four from the same office of a consulting company who work in four different sites on similar projects may have a standing conference call for a weekly update. A conference call, however, may be less effective if members of the team do not know each other or when new members join the team.

Preferring the Simple to the Complex The range of tools available for collaboration is wide and growing, but in deciding on an appropriate technology, be aware that dazzling features can turn counterproductive. They may

- intimidate potential participants.
- represent a form of technological imperialism to those less technically advanced.
- cost too much measured against the cost of a total project.
- consume vast amounts of time in installation and training.
- fail to accommodate incompatibilities among various sites for collaboration.
- break down unless attended to by well trained technicians.

For those reasons, choose the simplest technology that can get the job done. A small team may find that e-mail exchanges, perhaps on a targeted Listserv, are all it needs to accomplish its work. Larger teams or complex projects may require the more sophisticated applications available on the Web or on company intranets. These offer, for example, a secure space for posting such items as team biographies, drafts of project documents, and

Establish a baseline of shared beliefs.

- Openly discuss fundamental questions.
- Examine differences and areas of potential conflict.
- Take time from direct work on the project to resolve differences and nurture processes.

Build trust and credibility.

- Pay attention to how you are perceived by others.
- Deliver on promises.
- Deal straightforwardly with colleagues.
- Respond promptly to e-mails and voice mails.
- Perform team tasks reliably.

Participate in a shared workspace.

- Establish a virtual team room, a way to meet, a routine for all to share in developing ideas and communication products.
- Implement procedures for the use of the space and for informing teammates about progress.

Communicate frequently and appropriately.

Figure 11.3 Developing the Virtual Team

Source: Based in part on Deborah J. Barrett's adaptation of Richard Benson-Armer and Tsun-yan Hsieh, "Teamwork Across Time and Space," *The McKinsey Quarterly*, 1997, No. 4, 18–27.

updates from each team member; a scheduling function that automatically determines from data entered by team members the best time for a virtual meeting and sends notices of the meeting; and a chat room where team members can brainstorm (see Chapter 5).

Building Team Identity

Besides paying attention to its technology, the virtual team also needs to pay attention to itself *as* a team, creating explicitly a baseline of shared beliefs and trust, with more attention needed the greater the cultural differences between team members (Figure 11.3 and Figure 7.2). Without overemphasizing those differences, the team needs to surface them, from the relatively superficial (like accommodating every member's local holidays and work hours in the schedule) to deeper differences in local policies, ideologies, and practices. People from different cultures often have different approaches to solving problems, setting goals, dealing with (or not dealing with) conflicts, apportioning tasks, and the like.

In addition, the team may represent different levels of management, or include representatives of a client, or otherwise incorporate individuals who are not each other's peers. Those differences in roles and responsibilities need to be accounted for at the beginning of the project. For example, will the person of the highest rank automatically control the technology and thus team procedures? How will the team foster the contributions of lower-ranking members? How will the team ensure—if this is necessary—that the client's representative will make appropriate use of any proprietary information? The team's operating charter (see Chapter 10) should incorporate statements and guidelines that recognize and accommodate these differences in culture or position among team members.

The charter should also indicate who has access to what documents. A team manager may decide to restrict access on a need-to-know basis to maintain security or to foster efficiency. Financial experts, for example, look only at financial information, marketing experts at sections that deal with sales. Such restrictions keep members from squandering their attention on documents that don't require it. A permission system (sometimes called "message history") can also track usage, indicating who is working on a file at a given time, who has downloaded the file (and when), how many times an individual has downloaded the file, and how many times in total all members of the team have worked with the file.

Conducting Virtual Meetings

Even the heartiest supporters of technology acknowledge the limits of digital workspaces and digital work. When possible, a team should meet in person, face to face, to build relationships at the beginning of a project; reinforce those bonds at the end of a project, especially a successful one; and aid in resolving conflicts and enhancing consensus during a project (see Chapter 10). It's harder to negotiate online than in person. Misunderstandings often remain uncorrected for a longer period in a series of e-mails than in a face-to-face conversation. In addition, working electronically often builds motivation to meet in person the people whose e-mail messages you have been reading.

Face-to-face meetings, however, may be difficult and expensive to arrange—and they may not always be necessary. Electronic versions can accomplish many of the same goals. In the middle of a project, such meetings help accomplish straightforward, productivity-oriented tasks. Three common technologies for virtual meetings are audio conferences, online meetings, and videoconferences.

Audio Conferences

The simplest virtual meeting is a conference call or a conversation using a speaker phone. Participants at remote locations are connected in real time but without any visual reinforcement of the people or documents in the discussion. Conference calls can foster brainstorming as the team scopes out a project and negotiates a schedule. They can also help the team stay in touch, providing an occasion for more direct interactivity and spontaneity than, for example, e-mail messages. You hear actual voices. But because it is hard to talk about documents and visuals in the abstract, such calls are less helpful in the actual crafting of a final product. Poor speakers of the language of the call also may find it difficult to participate, and the other participants may lose patience with them. Figure 11.4 shows a protocol for a conference call or meeting by speaker phone.

Speaker-phone meetings and conference calls are easy to arrange and make low technical demands on the participants. They are particularly good at connecting teams of up to five people who know each other well. To perform effectively, however, participants have to pay special attention. One seasoned manager says he always stands when he is on a conference call; he thinks he projects better, has more sense of control. If you're invisible to the other participants, it's easy to slouch, and that

Moderator

Circulates in advance, usually via e-mail:

- Logistics: date, time, expected duration of the call, appropriate phone numbers.
- An agenda, which lists first the items that require everyone and then allows individuals to hang up when their participation is no long needed.
- Talking points.
- Any short text that will be the subject of discussion.
- A list of participants.

Appoints a note taker and rotates that task at different meetings.

Opens the discussion and sets a time limit.

Introduces each participant as she or he joins the conversation or asks participants to introduce themselves.

Makes sure everyone who is listening to the call is introduced.

Announces the procedure for turn taking (for example, that everyone will make a two-minute statement followed by a one-minute question from each participant, in the order of their introduction).

Brings any nonactive participants gently into the conversation by direct request ("Sam, what do you think of Lisette's description?").

Allows participants a one-minute wrap-up.

Summarizes action items.

Schedules the next call, if appropriate, before ending.

Ends discussion on time.

Figure 11.4 | Protocol for an Audio Conference

makes your voice reveal an unengaged participant. It's also easy to try multitasking—performing routine work during the call. But listening under such circumstances takes even more concentration than in a face-to-face meeting. If everyone multitasks, the whole process slows down.

Online Meetings

A second technology for virtual meetings uses Internet- or intranet-connected personal computers (PCs) or personal digital assistants (PDAs) to, as one application provider notes, "bring the meeting to you."

Participant

Identifies him/herself briefly before each comment ("Andy here") so that other participants know who is speaking and so that a tape of the conversation, if one is being made, can be transcribed with accurate attributions.

Speaks naturally, directly into the phone or toward the speaker phone.

Asks, if unsure about how one's voice is being received: "Am I too loud?" "Can you hear me?" Such questions, asked early in the conversation and not overused, help accommodate the limits of the technology.

Avoids side conversations (if two or more people are at one location).

Accommodates pauses. After a pause, prefaces remarks with an insertion phrase like, "Is it ok if I jump in here? This is Steve."

Follows the moderator's schedule if not needed for an entire session.

Mutes the speaker phone when not speaking.

Figure 11.4 Cont. Protocol for an Audio Conference

Chat Room One form of online meeting is a chat room. Similar to an instant messaging system, a chat room allows team members to log onto a site at the same time and type messages interactively to each other. It may stretch the meaning of "chat" when a team uses this technology to review security at company buildings worldwide or to brainstorm a proposal to a client, but the process does work, especially on a secure site and with a well established protocol for participant introductions, turn taking and the framing of messages, acceptable length of contributions, and the like. As with any electronic meeting, one advantage is the ability to quickly connect remote team members without the necessity of travel. In addition, those whose speaking skills are weak may find it more comfortable to type their messages. Team members can also upload texts for discussion, cut and paste messages for further follow-up, and direct messages to specific individuals rather than the whole group.

Users also cite several disadvantages:

- Speedy typists can dominate the conversation, and those who type more slowly may have a hard time getting attention.
- Similarly, participants with faster computers have an edge over those with slower download times.

- Non-native speakers of the chat room's dominant language may have more problems writing in that language than speaking it and thus may find themselves at a disadvantage.
- It's hard to incorporate the nuances of your position as you type. Contributions thus tend to be either more blunt or more bland than in face-to-face or phone-to-phone meetings.
- As with other virtual meetings, chat rooms raise issues of status and credibility. Participants have to establish these explicitly, through their self-introductions, their relative formality in style, and the content and length of their contributions.

Video- and Voice-Enhanced Applications More sophisticated electronic meeting applications integrate text, voice, video, and data. With audio cards and small cameras installed on each computer, meeting participants can see and hear each other and respond interactively. Video images of each participant can be streamed in a box or several boxes on all participants' screens. The cameras can also take photographs of documents and 3-D objects and project them to each linked computer. The advantage of these enhancements is the availability of further kinetic cues around the text. Many participants, however, especially those uncomfortable being photographed, mostly stand immobile and make little use of gestures. In addition, the camera provides only a narrow frame of reference.

As with a conference call, online meetings require the direction of a moderator or facilitator who orchestrates the interaction of participants, often by using special features of electronic meeting systems embedded in the software. The meeting moderator or facilitator, for example, can

- pose a question to the group (either by voice or by typing it onto the screen). She can then ask participants to respond to the question; the software will automatically display the responses.
- survey the group concerning their opinions on an issue or a course of action and display the results of the survey.
- take questions from the group. A "raised-hand" indicator allows participants to ask questions, and a queuing system automatically delivers the questions to the facilitator.
- upload documents or slides for discussion before the meeting or during the meeting.
- use an interactive white board to draw the results of a brainstorming session that will appear on each participant's screen. Participants, too, can draw on the board.

The software stores all information in a database that can be indexed. That record provides a rapid departure point for any action step decided on in the meeting.

Videoconferences

A third option for virtual meetings is a dedicated electronic conference room connected by satellite to other such rooms across the globe. This technology comes close to offering the advantages of face-to-face meetings among team members at remote locations. Where meetings by networked personal computers serve individual team members, several team members at a time can be accommodated in a conference room. This technology works well for large projects with several team members in each organization. It also accommodates, for example, a meeting between a team at the office and one or more individual members reporting from the field. Participants are videod at each location, in real time, and that video provides the illusion of everyone's being in a room at once, with the availability of body language and voice cues. The video is displayed on a large, flat computer panel. Documents, too, can be displayed and annotated, either by all participants in turn or by one designated individual who adjusts the document to reflect all participant contributions.

But video display does not fully compensate for drawbacks of any virtual meeting:

- Even in high-quality resolution, people are still images and can be cut off by the camera's frame.
- Some words will be mumbled or otherwise lost in transmission.
- If the meeting is conducted in a language many participants speak as a second language, then accents may impede others' comprehension.
- Similarly, pauses for translation when the meeting is conducted in more than one language may distract remote participants.

However, the technology does offer the opportunity for a face-to-face meeting at one site to incorporate a larger group in virtual form. As a participant, you need to balance your attention between those in the room with you and those on the screen, giving those on the screen at least equal time (Figure 11.5).

Prepare

Distribute logistical and project information well before the meeting.

Prepare slides or documents:
- bold type, at least 14 point
- landscape mode
- wide margins, free of text

Preview slides and charts on the document camera.

Avoid wearing white clothing, flashy jewelry, or busy patterns.

Practice with the equipment.

Arrange for a technician on standby, at least for the early minutes of the conference, in addition to the conference manager.

Develop a code to briefly identify each site on camera.

Perform

As with an audio conference, introduce all participants (probably best done by the conference manager), first at the site and then remotely.

Encourage participation through polling and questioning.

Rotate among the sites in a predetermined sequence and check off each site before proceeding to the next.

Provide enough time for each site to read any visuals or documents being presented.

Adjust the camera to zoom, pan, and otherwise show as much of each site and of individuals as possible.

Mute the microphone between speakers.

Accommodate fatigue; take breaks.

In an open discussion (no more than three sites), if two sites begin to speak at once, let the manager interrupt to designate the speaking order.

Figure 11.5 Protocol for a Videoconference

Source: Based in part on "Tips and Techniques for Audio Conference Calls," available at www.att.com/conferencing/tip_vid.html.

Staying in Touch Via E-Mail

Whatever other technology the virtual team incorporates into its workspace, one essential component is e-mail (for more advice on e-mail, see Chapter 8).

Advantages and Disadvantages

E-mail has many advantages in collaborative processes, as you've undoubtedly discovered:

- *It balances the participants.* Those reluctant to speak up in a teleconference may find their voice more easily in an e-mail message. Those who talk too much at meetings may write too much, too, but their e-mail can be skimmed.
- *It removes the time pressure of a phone call,* especially for non-native speakers who may need more time to compose and read messages.
- *It accommodates reading across time zones.* E-mail allows team members around the globe to write and read at times appropriate to them. Work can be smoothly handed off as the sun rises and sets from east to west.
- *It encourages brevity.* Although some people complain about this feature, e-mail does provide an opportunity for almost contextless, one- or two-sentence messages. As team members develop a shared understanding of the project and each other, messages can be minimal and still work.

The disadvantages are also rather well known, especially pressures to move toward a 24-hour workday, not just for the team as a whole but for each team member. Those minimalist messages may also strike readers as brusque; small misunderstandings or offenses tend to expand through the back and forth of messages on e-mail and may require a phone call or face-to-face meeting to correct.

Guidelines

Here are a few guidelines for reaping the advantages and reducing the disadvantages of e-mail as a way to stay in touch on a team:

- Compose specific project-oriented subject lines that stand out in an in-box index. Use a project code or number (or both) for openers—

and keep that consistent. Follow it with a key word or two indicating the particular message you're sending now:

Re: Adams Project. Follow up on Steve's list of tasks

- Similarly, create file names for attachments that distinguish drafts from each other and project documents from other documents that the reader may receive. Dates and author names are also useful:

  Johnson report. Version 3. 25 Feb 2003. Smith

- As with any group project, determine (the manager may do this) the sequence of messages (see Chapter 10). Will all e-mails go to one designated writer? To the manager? To everyone on the project? To your subgroup? The decision should reflect the team's agreed-on process along with a generally conservative principle: send messages only to those who really need them.
- Decide, as a team or as the manager, about the management of the team's active in-box of team messages. Each individual can probably delete most project correspondence regularly, perhaps automatically, at the end of a set period. If a team member has a reason to save some items, he or she can create an electronic folder for them. In addition, comply with any company policy about long-term retention of project e-mails.

As a team, agree on a protocol for response time to messages (see Chapter 8). Information technology tends to enhance the pressure to respond rapidly. That pressure can exacerbate tensions among team members when some *don't* respond or use silence as a disarming communication strategy. You'll need to agree on timing—on how you'll determine which messages require which speed of response. Agree, too, on any sanction to be imposed on nonresponsive teammates.

Annotating Drafts

Virtual meetings and e-mail messages help the team to develop ideas and shape its communication products. In a third approach to virtual teamwork, participants annotate, that is, comment on, the drafts of documents or slides circulated by e-mail or posted on a digital workspace. These annotations take two broad forms: on-the-line editing and more substantive comments about organization, priorities in presentation, appropriateness to

Guidelines for Reviewing

Be brief. Just because a dialog box expands to contain anything you say, don't feel required to be expansive.

Be precise. Read the text, visuals, and numbers carefully to note obvious errors, like columns in a percentage chart that don't add up to 100 percent or discrepancies between information in the text and that in a visual.

Be specific and concrete (not "This segment doesn't work." but "Maybe you need to define *revenue* here." "Shouldn't 'tourism' and 'financial services' both be first-level headings and segments?").

Control the impulse to rewrite unless you've been specifically asked to do so.

Praise good work. Create *positive* as well as negative comments ("Nice analysis and explanation here!").

Remember the team. Frame comments in terms of "we" rather than "you."

Be sensitive, especially with people who might be embarrassed about their writing skills, who are writing in a second language, or who may have been brought up to avoid open criticism and confrontation.

Use the concept of triage. As emergency personnel sequence patients for care based on the acuteness of their condition, focus on major issues, on required changes rather than personal preferences.

Figure 11.6 | Guidelines for Reviewing

the audience, and the like (see Chapters 8 and 9). The annotations may address only the principal writer, or they may become the occasion for a series of follow-up remarks by all team members, a process often called "reviewing" (Figure 11.6).

The reviewing techniques reflect the technology that delivers drafts to the team. Reviewers of short documents distributed by e-mail may simply write their comments within the text of the original message in another typeface or capital letters. Reviewers of very long documents distributed or posted as read-only .pdf files may create e-mail messages with their comments or contribute to a virtual workspace chat room. Two other techniques are the "track changes" option and online annotation.

Quality isn't an add-on. It's ~~something~~ inherent in the processes and products of a company,~~ it's something that~~ and may be hard to define concretely.,~~ but~~ O~~o~~ur customers, however, know when our products are quality products and when they are not. And we know if our processes are organized in a way to produce quality. Let's talk a bit about how our processes lead to quality in our products.

Figure 11.7 | An Example of Text with Annotations Highlighted Through the "Track Changes" Option

Tracking Changes

The "track changes" option in Microsoft Word® allows a reviewer to mark up copy, deleting or adding text and making comments in boxes that open when desired. The original text is maintained, although a reader, invoking the option, can also see the changes. The changes can accumulate as different readers add their responses (generally, in a box that is headed with a note identifying the reviewer, although that feature can be turned off if the team prefers anonymous review). Figure 11.7 shows a section of a document with changes. Any word could also be marked for a comment box, which covers the original text when it is opened but otherwise resides behind the text.

Annotating Online

Digital workspaces on the Web also offer the option of online annotation (Figure 11.8). Markers, often small pictures of the people making the comments, indicate where text is being commented on, and that text is highlighted. Participants make their annotations in a dialog box that allows for original comments as well as follow-ups. Users view the comments in a pop-up "quick viewer" or as a separate page.

Capturing the Team's Knowledge

During any project, and especially at its end, the team should capture the knowledge it has gained about its processes (see Chapter 10). This step is especially important for virtual teams. They should assess the role of

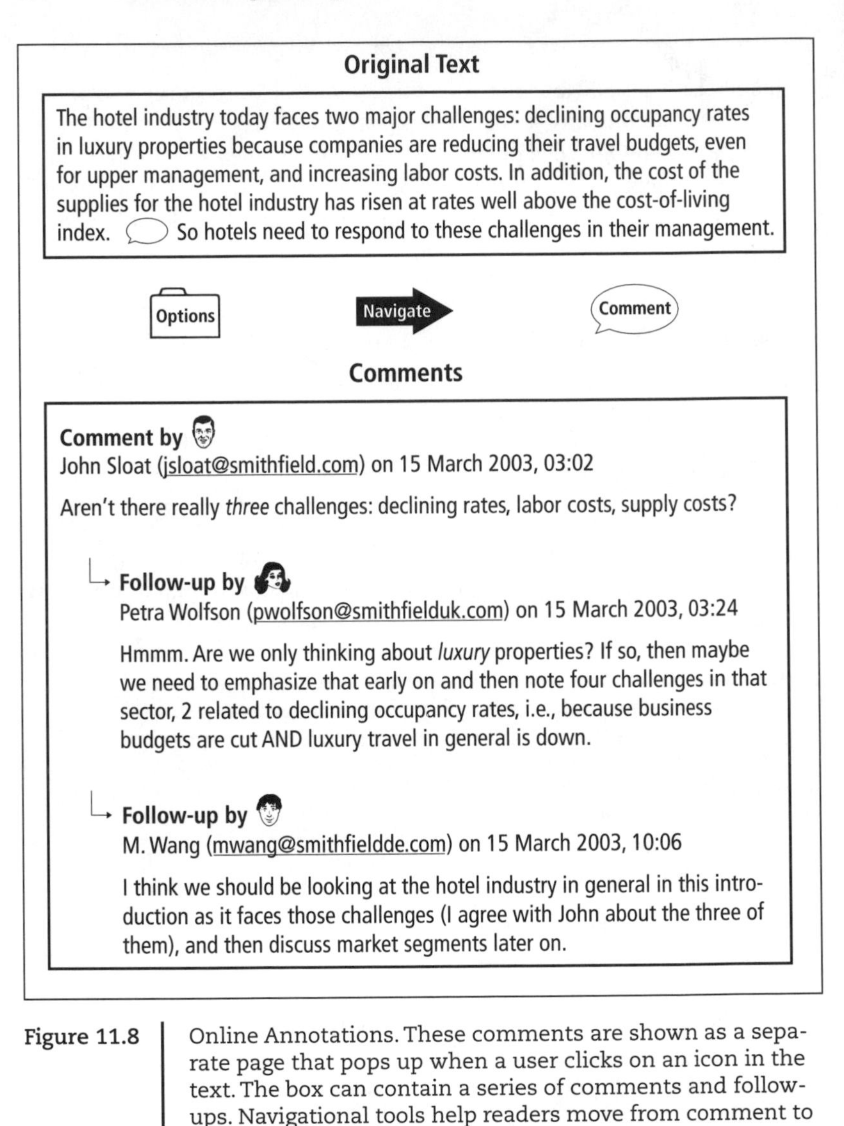

Figure 11.8 Online Annotations. These comments are shown as a separate page that pops up when a user clicks on an icon in the text. The box can contain a series of comments and follow-ups. Navigational tools help readers move from comment to comment and through sections of the text, each identified by its heading.

technology in their work to decide on any changes necessary to make that technology more robust, or less invasive, or more supportive. That knowledge can improve future work, whether the team stays together or, more likely, disbands. Members then bring that knowledge to new teams and new situations.

In addition, the team needs to attend to the record of messages and products that working digitally automatically creates. It's a much more extensive record than is common for projects conducted mostly in person. Although the minutes of face-to-face meetings, for example, may run to a page or two, the record of an online meeting includes every message anyone typed. Similarly, workspace software stores e-mail messages and in-text annotations.

To take advantage of this record, and to avoid being overwhelmed by it, the team needs to decide early in the project

- what *messages* go into an archive, and for how long.
- what *drafts* can be deleted as they are replaced by later versions.
- whether *contrary opinions and objections* to a final decision should be given a place in the record, and if so, in what form.

In an increasingly litigious United States, and with increasingly close ties between U.S. companies and others across the globe, that project record may also become subject to close legal scrutiny, by the government or by regulatory boards of any number of nations. Thus records must be kept with that oversight in mind, especially if the project is at all controversial or unusual. Teams also need to conform rigorously to any company policies concerning the retention and shredding or deleting of documents; in multiple company projects, the most conservative policy should apply.

All of these guidelines assume that team members have equal access to a common and high-end computing infrastructure. To the degree that your team brings together individuals without access to such systems, or with only sporadic access, you'll need to make allowances. It's easy to assume that your (probably pretty sophisticated) system is universal. Don't be trapped by such an assumption.

SCENARIO

Using Technology to Communicate Globally

Like most U.S. retailers who experience a holiday sales boost, the catalog company where Connie Park was vice president for purchasing and supply-chain management had its best sales in the final quarter of the calendar year. Gross sales increased 18 percent over the year-earlier period. Unfortunately, canceled orders increased from 4 percent of total sales to 9 percent. There were two sources for the canceled orders: order mistakes (that is, sending the wrong item, size, or color, which resulted in a return) and lack of inventory to meet a customer's order at the time the item was requested. Canceled orders obviously reduce gross sales and thus profit margins. Additionally, they increase costs because of the time needed to process them and deal with customers, and they also harm the company's image and reduce repeat buying.

"This is unacceptable," the president of the catalog retailer said to Connie and to Wayne Pascarella, vice president for sales and marketing, when the three of them met in January to review sales and canceled orders reports for the past quarter. "Canceled orders are killing us—and they're growing. What are you going to do to fix the problem?"

Connie and Wayne promised an answer within a week.

"You want to run this?" Wayne asked Connie after they left the meeting with the president. "It seems like a supply issue, and that's your area."

Connie knew that supply-chain management (SCM) was indeed part of the problem and under her control. SCM included supervision of buying and the coordination of production and shipping schedules to make sure inventory at the store's fulfillment centers was adequate to meet orders in a timely fashion. Peter Spyros was director of SCM. Because the company sourced many of its products internationally, another executive—Suzanne Laberge, director of international sourcing, who also reported to Connie—was involved. But SCM and sourcing were only part of the problem. Canceled orders could be reduced only through close coordination with the sales function so that the inventory would be available at the right time to meet customer orders. The manager of customer fulfillment oversaw the company's call centers where orders were placed and its fulfillment centers from which the orders were shipped. Identifying and solving the problems that led to the increase in canceled orders therefore required the help of the manager of customer fulfillment, Glen Finegold, who reported to Wayne.

"I don't mind taking the lead," Connie told Wayne, "but I'll need Glen on this because it's a fulfillment issue, too."

"I'll tell him right away," Wayne said. "If you need me, let me know. Unless I hear otherwise, I'll assume Glen is giving you all the support you need from our side."

Connie Park convened the team that afternoon: Peter Spyros (SCM), Suzanne Laberge (international sourcing), and Glen Finegold (customer fulfillment), with Connie as lead member. She established two goals: to identify what had gone wrong in the fourth quarter that had led to the increase in canceled orders, and to put in place an operational strategy to coordinate purchasing, production, and shipping with customer orders and order fulfillment. Then she asked for comments.

"It's because we're all over the place—all over the world, really," Peter said. "We source 85 percent of our goods from abroad, we have customer call centers in India and Ireland, and our fulfillment centers are in Maryland and Utah. Meanwhile, we're all here in Pittsburgh. That's why things break down."

"With all the money we spend on telecommunications," Connie said, "we shouldn't have problems just because our operations are dispersed."

"Maybe we spend money but still don't communicate," Suzanne interjected.

"Maybe so," Glen said, "but it seems to me we've really got to communicate now—to find out where we went wrong."

"And how we're going to operate differently in the future," Connie added. "I agree—we've got to look at both sides of the chain—the supply piece and the customer piece—and find out what happened. We've got to talk to the people who know what's happening—regardless of where they are. You folks know the technology better than I do. How should we proceed?"

"Worldwide videoconference at the end of the week," Glen said. "With everyone who reports to Suzanne, Peter, and me."

"Maybe we could send an e-mail to all of them, with some questions," Suzanne said.

"Before, or instead of the videoconference?" Connie asked.

"Before. Then we could figure out whether we need the videoconference," Suzanne answered. "Or I suppose we could set up a chat room and see what happens when everyone gets going."

"Maybe we should all just call our direct-reports," Peter said. "See what we can find out that way before we get everyone in chat rooms and videoconferences and e-mail. I think you need to *talk* to people sometimes—real people, real conversation."

The three executives turned to Connie to see which route she wanted to follow.

"Let's jump ahead a few steps," she told them. "I'm trying to imagine how we can get better coordination among all the groups, and as you've been suggesting how to do that as we look for the problems, I'm wondering if we should just *assume* that the problem is poor communication and fix that right away. Let's say we set up a daily conference call among the principals from SCM, sourcing, and customer fulfillment. Get them talking, comparing notes about customer interests, purchasing, shipping, everything. Instead of focusing on a problem, we'd be focusing them on solutions. During the calls we could probably spot what went wrong last quarter, but we'd already be on our way to fixing things instead of making people feel guilty about what went wrong."

"Why a conference call?" Glen asked. "Why not a videoconference, so people could see each other?"

"We could do that," Connie answered. "But it's a lot more complicated, and we'd have to get people into the facilities, whereas if we go with a call some of them can be on their mobile phones from home or wherever."

"What about the time differences?" Suzanne asked.

"That's why they have mobile phones," Connie said. "Any other comments?"

"I still think we should make some phone calls first," Peter said. "And stick with the problem before we jump to the solution."

"What's our goal here?" Glen asked. "Getting information for a report, or getting people to talk so we can fix the problem?"

"Both," Connie said.

"Okay, you're the boss, Connie," Peter said.

"Well, not *my* boss," Glen said, "but I agree with Connie. Let's set up a conference call for tomorrow. Then we can see if we can do a videoconference after that, maybe rotate the two over the next few weeks and just see what happens."

Questions for Discussion

1. How is the team established? Are the right people on it? Would another approach to assembling the team be helpful? If so, in what ways?

2. Are there any potential problems with having Connie lead the team? Should Wayne be a coleader because he is parallel to Connie in the organization? Are there any problems with having Glen Finegold as a member when he doesn't report to Connie?
3. Evaluate the various forms of technological collaboration proposed, identifying their strengths and weaknesses as means of getting information and developing a strategy: e-mail, individual phone calls, conference call, videoconference. Which would you recommend—and why? Does the group evaluate the technologies systematically to find the right fit?
4. Does the geographic dispersion of discussion participants create problems? How do the various technologies address those problems? On balance, which will work best?
5. Are the two goals Glen points out—using collaborative technology to *communicate* about the issues (i.e., to identify problems and establish solutions) and using it for operational purposes—compatible?
6. Is Connie making a mistake by mixing identification of the problem with its solutions? Might her decision to "jump ahead" cause later problems?
7. How should Connie explain the purposes of the virtual meetings to those involved? Suggest what she should say to the group when it's assembled.
8. How should the working group document its efforts? How should it capture the knowledge it gains through the communication process?

PART

III Appendixes

APPENDIX **A** Conventions of Language and Usage

APPENDIX **B** Conventions of Format

APPENDIX **C** Dealing with the Public and Crisis Communication

APPENDIX

Conventions of Language and Usage

Effective management communication follows conventions of language and usage. Three aspects of these conventions are covered in this appendix: inclusive language, sentence construction, and punctuation.

The conventions described here are common in standard American English. Although American English is used in business worldwide, you should be alert to differences between it and other Englishes, especially British, particularly with regard to punctuation and spelling.

In addition, be aware that some corporations establish their own conventions that override the standards described here. For example, some businesses, to appear friendly, mandate that letters to customers use a comma instead of a colon to follow the greeting ("Dear Ms. Jones,"). If that is your company's official style, follow it. In British English, the comma is generally used after a greeting, even in formal letters.

Conventions should be viewed as aids rather than impediments to communication. Without standards, you can drift, waste time, or make errors. Following them eases your job as a communicator.

Inclusive Language

The words you select as you write and speak should reflect the multicultural reality of management. Think of this as the linguistic version of free trade: select words that reflect awareness of the global community in which you operate; words that lower rather than raise barriers; words that include rather than exclude; words that show no bias with respect to one's race, sex, age, national or ethnic origin, or physical or mental condition. Prefer words that reflect inclusion and avoid words that reflect bias.

Prefer	**Avoid**
Nongendered titles:	**Gendered titles:**
businessperson	businessman
flight attendant	stewardess
waitperson	waiter or waitress
police	policeman
chair	chairman, chairwoman
***He/she*, a mix of pronouns, or *they* (for plural subjects)**	**Exclusive use of *he* or *she***
Non-"centric" descriptions of countries or people:	**"Centric" descriptions:**
Asian	Oriental, Eastern
European, North American, South American	Western
Neutral descriptions of characteristics:	**Stereotypical descriptions:**
Tall/short	Giant/dwarf
Disabled/challenged	Crippled
Senior	Elderly
Fit	Able bodied
Visually impaired	Blind

Be alert for unconscious bias. If you write "the doctor should consider the impact of delays on his patients" or "the nurse should be sure her notes are in order," you imply that doctors are men and nurses are women. You may not mean that, but such language reinforces gender stereotypes with respect to professions. Similarly, avoid words like "nonwhite" to describe groups—why should "white" be the default? Bandages are often described as "flesh-colored," an inappropriate description if an African or Asian person is applying the pink ones typical in the United States. Such examples reflect the pervasiveness of noninclusive language and the consequent need to be alert to words or phrases that fail to recognize the diversity and multiculturalism of business.

Conventions of Sentence Structure

The primary building block of text is the sentence. A sentence shows a completed thought about an actor and some action or about a state of being, along with possible modifiers of the actor, the action, or the state of being. Every sentence has an actor (or subject) and a statement about that actor (a verb). Making such a statement about a subject is called *predication*. For example:

> Sales improved for the quarter.

Here, "sales" is the subject, and "improved" is the verb. "For the quarter" modifies "improved," telling *when* sales improved.

As you write, keep in mind the simple definition that every sentence has an actor and an action. Who is doing what? You can add complications like "to whom?" and "when?" and "under what circumstances?" and "with what results?" But don't let those complications drown the actor or (more commonly) the action. Welcome short, pithy sentences that clearly show who is doing what.

To write or speak within the conventions of the sentence, be especially aware of *active voice, agreement, completion, expletives, modification,* and *parallelism.*

Active Voice

Predication can be in the active or passive voice. The voice is active if the subject does the acting; it is passive if the subject is acted upon. This is active:

> The auditors refused to permit the recognition of revenue from the long-term contract.

This is passive:

> Revenue recognition from the long-term contract was not permitted.

The active voice is generally preferred because it shows clearly who did what. The passive tends to obscure the identity of the actor. The passive voice is acceptable when you are trying to avoid identifying an actor (for example, when legal considerations suggest the need to avoid saying who did what to whom) or when there is no clear actor ("rainwater was absorbed gradually into the dry land"). But most management communication should be in the active voice. If you do employ the passive, do so only for a known reason.

Agreement

Subjects and verbs—actors and actions—must agree in number. Single subjects require singular verbs, and plural subjects require plural verbs. For example:

The nature of their cost calculations were unknown.

In this sentence, the subject is "nature," a singular noun. Because "calculations" comes just before the verb, it's easy—but wrong—to think it's the subject and therefore use a plural verb. To make the agreement correct, write

The nature of their cost calculations was unknown.

It may be better in this case to make "calculations" the subject to produce a crisper sentence:

Their cost calculations were unknown.

But notice that this form carries a different meaning. You have to decide whether the "nature" of the calculations or the "calculations" themselves are unknown.

Completion

A sentence must have complete predication. This is not a sentence:

John being aware of the falloff in revenues.

"Being aware" is not a completed form of action. (Because of the incom plete verb form, such constructions are often called "fragments" or "sentence fragments.") Instead, write

John was aware of the falloff in revenues.

Expletives

The constructions "there is," "there are," and "it is" are called expletives. We use them commonly in speech: "There is no way I'll do that," or "It's obvious that the products are faulty." But avoiding expletives in business writing sharpens sentences and makes meaning clearer. Here is a poor use of the expletive form:

There are many possible solutions known to our sales force to correct this problem.

A better sentence results from avoiding the expletive, identifying the actors, and using a strong verb:

Our sales force knows many possible solutions for this problem.

Sometimes expletives are delayers, used in speech while you try to focus on what you want to say:

> It is a generally held belief that top-line revenue growth trumps expense reduction as a long-term strategy.

Without the expletive construction, you can make the point more succinctly:

> Top-line revenue growth trumps expense reduction as a long-term strategy.

Modification

Words and phrases can modify both the actor and the action in a sentence. For example:

> Moving slowly, Maria reorganized the division with great care.

Here "moving slowly" modifies "Maria," and "with great care" modifies "reorganized." Modifiers are useful, but they have an annoying tendency to dangle, or to be misplaced. A dangling modifier is a phrase that usually comes at the beginning or end of a sentence and denotes an action that the subject of the sentence isn't capable of. Here is a dangling modifier:

> Having completed the reorganization, sales increased.

When you place the modifying phrase "having completed the reorganization" immediately before "sales," you are saying that "sales" somehow did the acting—that is, completed the reorganization. This is of course not logical since "sales" in this sense is not capable of performing a reorganization. Instead, you could write

> Sales increased after the division was reorganized.

Better still, avoid the passive voice and identify (and give credit to) the actor who did the reorganizing:

> After the vice president completed the reorganization, sales increased.

Like a dangling modifier, a misplaced modifier appears in the wrong place in a sentence and so modifies the wrong word. Unlike the dangling modifier, the misplaced one can't be easily spotted based on the use of an offsetting comma. Here is a misplaced modifier:

> Rodriquez questioned how many additional security guards were necessary at the beginning of the meeting.

One presumes that the *guards* were not necessary at the beginning of the meeting but rather that Rodriquez raised his question then. Dangling and misplaced modifiers can create humor, at the author's expense. For example:

> My client has discussed your proposal to fill the drainage ditch with his partners.

Obviously—one hopes—the proposal isn't to use the partners as fill. Put the modifying phrase in the right place:

> My client has discussed with his partners your proposal to fill the drainage ditch.

Parallelism

Items in a list or series should be equal to each other in both logic and expression (see Chapter 5 and 6). When they are, we say they are parallel. When they are not, the fault is called lack of parallelism. Here is a sentence in which the elements of the list are not logically equal:

> There is to be no smoking, eating, or beverages in the conference room.

"Smoking" and "eating" are logically equal because they are activities; "beverage" refers to a specific item. The writer of this sentence was probably trying to avoid writing

> There is to be no smoking, eating, or drinking in the conference room.

While this version is parallel, the implications of "drinking" are probably not what the writer intended. A better version that is both parallel and direct (and avoids the expletive form "there is") is

> Do not smoke, eat, or drink any beverages in the conference room.

Here is another sentence that lacks parallelism:

> Medical services that are not available to employees in the clinic include X-rays, cuts and lacerations requiring sutures, broken bones, and any ailment requiring hospitalization.

Each item in the list should be what the subject describes—"medical services." Only X-rays qualify as that. Cuts, lacerations, broken bones, and ailments requiring hospitalization are not "medical services" but conditions that may require such services. This revision restores parallelism and expresses the point more directly:

> The clinic is not able to provide treatment for broken bones, cuts and lacerations that require sutures, or any other ailment requiring hospitalization.

Conventions of Punctuation

Punctuation helps you know when to pause or stop or pay special attention to words or phrases. Here, in alphabetical order, are the common punctuation marks used in English.

Apostrophe

An apostrophe (') shows possession. We write

The company's balance sheet is quite strong.

The apostrophe indicates that the balance sheet belongs to the company. If the subject possessing the item is plural, we put the apostrophe after the "s":

The three companies' balance sheets are all quite strong.

An apostrophe should not be used to form a plural (as in "three MBA's"). Instead, use just an "s" ("three MBAs").

Colon

A colon (:) can serve two purposes: (1) to begin a list (as we just did) and (2) to follow a greeting in a letter ("Dear Ms. Izawa:"). Note that in British English, a comma follows a greeting. Rarely, the colon can also be used to separate two independent clauses in a sentence if balance or contrast is intended ("The causes of the shortfall were well known: the remedies were not.")

Comma

A comma (,) sets off an introductory phrase ("Moving with slow and careful steps, the bank reviewed and eventually wrote down some nonperforming assets."); separates items in a list ("A balance sheet includes assets, liabilities, and shareholder equity."); or follows a greeting in an *informal* letter or e-mail ("Dear Herb,").

A comma should never be used to separate two independent clauses in a sentence ("She was going to get the numbers, he was opposed to finding out what really happened."). Instead, use a semicolon or dash, or separate the two clauses into two sentences ("She was going to get the numbers. He was opposed to finding out what really happened.").

Dash

The dash (—; created by using two hyphens in word processing programs) is used informally in place of the colon to introduce a list:

> Several items need to be considered—size, color, and weight.

The dash can also replace the semicolon to separate two independent clauses in a sentence:

> Each proposal had merit—neither was obviously superior.

Both of these uses are informal. In formal writing, avoid the dash.

Exclamation Point

The exclamation point (!) indicates excitement or enthusiasm. It is not conventional in formal writing, but it does appear in e-mail and informal notes.

Hyphen

The hyphen (-) connects multiword modifiers (e.g., half-baked or late-blooming). Do not use it when the first word is an adverb—that is, ends in "-ly." Don't write "slowly-moving," but do write "slow-moving."

Italics (or underlining)

Italic type (*italic*) is usually used for the titles of books or journals. Underlining is also commonly used, but word processing programs provide access to italic type itself. Italics or underlining can also be used—but always with caution—to show emphasis ("This is the *third* time I've had to remind you.").

Parenthesis

The parenthesis (( )) sets off parenthetic information—information that expands or explains:

> Staff members from all offices (accounting, finance, treasury) attended the meeting.
>
> Select appropriate categories (for example, under-20, 21–30, etc.) for the study.

Period

The period (.) ends a complete sentence.

Question Mark

The question mark (?) ends an interrogatory sentence, one that asks a question:

> Do we have the right information for this presentation?

Quotation Marks

Quotation marks ("/") indicate the exact words that someone speaks or writes:

> John asked, "Do we have the right information for this presentation?"

In American English, double marks are always used first, with single marks used within quotations:

> Maria asked, "What do we mean when we say 'standard' procedures?"

In British English, single marks are used first, with double marks used within quotations.

Notice that the question mark appears within the quotation marks. In British English, however, the period and question mark appear outside the quotation marks.

Quotation marks are also used to call attention to specific words:

> When we say "standards," we refer to GAAP.

They also indicate titles of articles in journals or newspapers:

> You should read the article in today's *Wall Street Journal,* "Avoiding Mistakes in Hiring."

Semicolon

The semicolon (;) separates two independent clauses:

> We were ready for the presentation; we were not ready for the reaction.

It also separates items in a list when commas or parentheses are used within the separated items:

> The data included market research, which was substantial; budget projections; and last year's profit statements.

Do not use the semicolon to introduce a list or to follow a greeting in a letter; the colon is the proper mark in those cases.

APPENDIX

B Conventions of Format

Follow your organization's format guidelines when you write a memo or letter. These formats may be embedded in a networked word processing system. For reports, follow any format requirements set by the audience; if a format isn't specified, then follow the format typical in your organization. This appendix provides common U.S. conventions for formatting memos, letters, and reports. Use these if you are writing on your own or if your company does not have a standard.

Memo

The standard heading of a memo (preset in most e-mail systems) includes four elements, usually in the following order:

Date:
To: (Name of one reader or a distribution list)
From: (You—your name and perhaps your title)
Subject: (Title of your message, key words)

Most e-mail systems and preprinted memo forms also include a cc line in the header (carbon copy) to name secondary readers. E-mail systems also allow you to create a "rich" header to, for example, send "blind carbon copies." Use this function when you send a message to many recipients. It saves readers the need to scroll through long mailing lists and protects the privacy of the list. To sign a print memo, depending on your relationship with the reader, either write your first name or initials on the "from" line (friendly) or sign at the end (more formal).

Memo Format

Date:
To:
Cc:
From:
Re:

Letter

The standard formats for U.S. letters are block, modified block, and simplified. The block is probably the most common, but some writers are fiercely loyal to the modified block because it seems more personal. The simplified format is sometimes considered brusque but works when you are writing to a role (like "Frequent Traveler Accounts" or "Refunds") or a P.O. Box (as in a response to a classified advertisement) and don't have a specific name to write to.

Adjust the top and bottom margins to center the image area of the letter on the page; if you have a short letter, don't leave the bottom two-thirds of the page blank. Left-justify the text, leaving the right margin ragged for ease of reading.

Standard letter elements:

1. **Heading.** Your address and date. Use your organization's letterhead or create your own.
2. **Inside address.** Name and address (postal or fax number) of recipient.
3. **Subject line.** Topic of the letter, project, or account number. The line is less common in a letter than in a memo.
4. **Salutation** (or attention line). The greeting. Generally, use "Dear," followed by the first name of the recipient and a comma (informal) or the full name and a colon (formal). Avoid "Dear Sir or Madam"; if you don't have a name, use an attention line for the role (Attention: Customer Service) or omit the salutation.
5. **Body.** The main message, in more than one paragraph. Generally, it is single-spaced, with double-spacing between paragraphs.
6. **Closing.** A conventional ending. Use "Sincerely yours" or "Yours truly" in a formal letter, "Respectfully yours" when you want to be more deferential, as in a cover letter to a proposal. Use "Best wishes" or "Warm regards" in a more personal letter.

7. **Signature**. Sign the letter as a mark of authorization, either above or below your typed name and title.
8. **Notations.** Initials of the typist, reference to an enclosure, names of people sent copies.

Block Letter Format

Every element begins at the left margin.

Letterhead

① Date

② Name
Company
Street Address
City, State, ZIP

③ Re:

④ Salutation:

⑤ And here we are

And here we are
And here we are

⑥ Closing

⑦ Signed signature
Typed signature

⑧ Cc:

Enc (1)

Modified Block Letter Format

Indent paragraphs five spaces (optional). Center date below letterhead or align with closing. Begin sender's address (if not letterhead), closing, and typed signature about seven tab stops across the page. Begin inside address, salutation, and any notations at the left margin.

Sender's Address ①

Date

② Name
Company
Street Address
City, State, ZIP

④ Salutation:

⑤ And here we are
And more and more

And here we are
And more and more

Closing ⑥

Signature ⑦
Typed signature

Simplified Letter Format

All elements begin at the left margin. No salutation or closing, although an attention or subject line is common.

Letterhead

① Date
② Inside Address (no personal name)

③ Re: *or* Attention:

⑤ And here we go

And here we go

⑦ Signature
Typed signature

Report

To give a report or proposal (see Chapter 8) full treatment, include the following ancillary elements around the core discussion:

Front Matter

Letter or Memo of Transmittal Presents and individualizes the report for a particular reader, reviews authorization and date, reminds the reader about any changes in scope in the project, acknowledges assistance, thanks the reader.

Title Page Title (of course—brief, clear, and comprehensive); names (and organization) of the author(s); name(s) (and organization) of the audience; date; and other necessary information about the report's origin and use. Use this as a design feature.

Table of Contents List of the report's headings, in order, followed by page numbers. If the report contains many figures or exhibits, consider creating a separate *list of figures*.

Executive Summary or Abstract The report in a nutshell: main points, main evidence, main recommendations or conclusions. It should make sense on its own because some readers will read only the summary, not the report. *Inform* the reader ("We recommend expansion into Montreal") rather than *describing* the report ("Our recommendation is given.").

Back Matter

Appendixes (if appropriate) Supplemental material not essential to the development of the report, including copies of questionnaires, extended tabulations summarized in the report, detailed quotations. Each appendix should be labeled with both a letter (A, B, C . . .) and a title.

References Full citations for any sources used in preparing your report.

Exhibits Tables, graphs, and other visuals that supplement materials in the report.

APPENDIX

Dealing with the Public and Crisis Communication

This book focuses on the communication processes and products integral to management—what managers do routinely to carry out their work. Sometimes managers must perform specialized communication tasks, either on their own or in tandem with communication specialists. Such tasks are not integrated with the management process but rather stand on their own. This appendix offers advice on two of these special communication situations: dealing with the public, and crisis communication.

The Manager's Expanded Role in Corporate Communication

Managers are increasingly involved in corporate communication because of two trends over the past decade. The first is a set of changes external to business organizations, and the second is internal, related to how organizations are structured and how they function.

The Mediazation of Society

The proliferation of news media (radio, cable and network TV, the Internet) and the attendant increased interest in finding and reporting stories have led to public scrutiny of matters formerly deemed too complex for the average viewer or listener. The media's search for scandals and other audience lures to fill the 24-hour news cycle has made highly public those issues that in the past attracted little media attention. Organizations as diverse as dot-com start-ups (or busts) and decades-old nonprofit charities now find themselves subject to media scrutiny. Although some lament this tendency, the wise manager should both recognize its reality and learn to exploit the opportunities it offers to communicate organizational messages.

Organic and Flattened Organizational Structures

As organizations are reshaped organically (with structures tied directly to organizational goals) or flattened (with reporting layers reduced), people take on wider responsibilities and with them a heightened sense of the need to know. Whereas older, more bureaucratic structures privileged top-down communication and internal secrecy, newer forms of organizing lead to a need for wider internal dissemination of information. The sharing of duties—fewer people taking on more responsibility and blurring lines between positions—triggers the sharing of information.

The Manager's Widened Communication Role

These two trends intersect to make formerly specialized communication functions more widely dispersed throughout businesses. Managers whose primary duties are operational are now called on to assist in—and sometimes even to take the lead in—communicating with the public and with others within the organization, tasks formerly reserved for designated professionals (in, for example, public, media, investor, and employee relations). The sales manager, head accountant, director of manufacturing, or MIS manager can no longer assume that communication is limited to preparing sales talks or writing memos, reports, and letters.

The advice in this appendix is not intended only for corporate communication specialists but rather for all managers who in their day-to-day responsibilities find they are called on to deal with external and internal audiences on both routine and unique communications. This advice is parallel to and compatible with the core advice about managerial communication presented in this guide. The processes of analysis, design, creation, and verification apply directly to the communication products of media relations and crisis communication. And because working managers who deal with the media and crises almost always do so with the aid of professionals in those fields, the processes of collaborative communication have special relevance. The analysis and advice provided in this guide simply take on different focuses when you deal with the public and manage crisis communication.

Dealing with the Public

As a manager, you may be called on to represent your organization to the public by shaping and delivering a specific organizational message. Sometimes you may deal directly with the public, as when you address a community group about your proposed plant expansion. Or you may deal with them through such media as a newspaper or TV station, as when you respond to a reporter's inquiry about your company's stand on an economic or a political issue.

Except in very small organizations, you will likely have the help of a communication specialist—someone designated (perhaps in addition to other duties) as your organization's spokesperson. He or she may be called the PR (for public relations) director, media director, or director of communication. Whatever the title, the person is in charge of dealing with the public on behalf of the organization. But it is unlikely he or she can function effectively without the help of all managers. That's why it's important for managers to understand the fundamentals of good corporate communication, as summarized in Figure C.1.

Most of these guidelines derive from common sense, but they also draw upon your general awareness of communication processes and func-

Guidelines for Managers to Achieve Effective Corporate Communication

- Know the facts and the context. If you don't know, find out. Never guess or speculate.
- Consistently deliver to all audiences a single clear message that is as simple and direct as the situation allows.
- Focus on the primary audience (using media representatives as gatekeepers to the public).
- Stay in your organizational role—identify your expertise and position and don't speak or write beyond it.
- Be responsive but not reactive or passive.
- Support and take direction from your organization's communication specialists.
- Respect the professionalism of media representatives.

Figure C.1 Guidelines for Managers to Achieve Effective Corporate Communication

tions. For example, the communication model (see Chapter 1) is as applicable to writing a media release as it is to preparing a sales presentation. Equally appropriate is the management communication process, because for any communication you need to identify outcomes, audiences, media, and timing. Some of the guidelines for effective corporate communication are unique to public communications (the last two in the chart, for example), but all are consistent with good communication practice.

Working with a communication specialist presents additional challenges. It's important to understand the different roles the general manager and the communication specialist play in the creation of corporate communication products. Figure C.2 summarizes these roles for several typical products.

For most products, the manager's job is to assist the specialist by providing both information and the context for understanding that information. For example, if a business is preparing to send a media release describing a new policy on support of community charities, the accounting

COMMUNICATION PRODUCT	MANAGER'S ROLES	COMMUNICATION SPECIALIST'S ROLES
Media release **Letter to external special-interest group** (e.g., shareholders, union, community or political groups) **Employee memo**	Provide information and context Review for accuracy	Organize and write Gain internal approval Distribute
Media conference or employee meeting	Brief the specialist Attend if needed and respond to questions if appropriate	Organize and preside over Call on managers for help with questions

Figure C.2 Corporate Communication Products in Which Managers May Be Involved

manager may be asked to prepare a summary of past giving. It's important that that person supply more than numbers. If the company made a large donation to United Way one year but returned to a lower level of support the next, it would be helpful to supply the context—for example, a flood or other natural disaster may have triggered the large gift. That needs to be explained to the communication specialist so she can be prepared to answer a natural question—or, better, to anticipate it by providing the explanation for the large gift in the original media release instead of waiting to be asked about it.

Managers and communication specialists need to work together to find the facts and provide the context for understanding them. The specialist writes the release, but he may ask managers who contributed information to review it for accuracy. In this role, you can use the advice given in Chapters 9 and 11 for collaborative editing. The specialist has final responsibility for the release, including getting whatever internal approvals are needed before distributing it.

Dealing with a Crisis

Businesses and other organizations have always been subject to disruptive, unexpected events that bring routine operations to a halt and require focused management attention. The "mediazation" of society and changes in organizational structure heighten the communication aspects of such events. In addition to disrupting operations, crises increasingly draw intense internal and external interest. Managing a corporate crisis now calls for managing the ways in which it is communicated, both to those inside and those outside the organization.

Examples of such crises are abundant, from disasters such as airplane and tanker crashes to accounting irregularities, insider dealing, excessive executive compensation, tainted products, toxic dumping, and discriminatory employment practices. There is no hard-and-fast definition of a crisis. One may say it is truly in the eyes of the beholder: the greater the potential impact on the organization's ability to survive, the more accurate is the "crisis" description—and the more energy, time, and executive focus are needed to deal with it. The Scenario in Chapter 10 describes a relatively low-level (and hence more easily manageable) crisis in the form of a corporate merger. Most crises calling for special communication strategies are, unlike planned mergers, unexpected events, but even expected events can require crisis treatment.

The guidelines for effective corporate communication (Figure C.1) apply in a crisis. In addition, several special guidelines also apply, as summarized in Figure C.3.

Guidelines for Crisis Communication

- Provide a consistent message to all audiences, both internal and external.
- Respond rapidly, as soon as all relevant facts and interpretations are known.
- Release all relevant information at the outset.
- Communicate with a single voice that represents the highest level of organizational authority.
- Emphasize solutions rather than problems—actions taken to correct a problem rather than the problem itself.
- Be aware of, but not crippled by, legal considerations such as future liability.

Figure C.3 | Guidelines for Crisis Communication

A crisis requires special attention to the consistency of messages delivered to internal and external audiences. Because a crisis affects employees as much as the public, people inside the organization need to be given the same information and interpretations as those outside. It is tempting to consider some matters as being "in the family" (that is, within the organization) and others appropriate to the outside. In practice, this simply doesn't work. Employees are both "inside" and "outside"—members of the family and members of various outside public groups. While more detailed information about, say, a toxic-waste spill might be available to operating personnel in the company, the basic information offered in media releases and internal documents must never be contradictory—or able to be interpreted in different ways.

Rapid response and the commitment to provide all known information at the outset of a crisis are requirements of effective crisis communication. Slow leaks are fatal. The best advice is to get out all relevant and reliable information at the beginning—and quickly, before the crisis becomes a media event. Later qualification, explanation, or clarification can be damaging.

The need for a single, high-level voice to articulate the consistent messages is especially acute in a crisis. Companies that push communication responsibility downward to a designated person in public relations instead of speaking through high-level officials send an inappropriate message about the significance of the event. In a true crisis, the person at the top, generally the chief executive officer, has to be the primary voice for all communication. Obviously, the messages he or she delivers are shaped by communication specialists with the close cooperation of all managers, but the voice needs to be singular and high level.

It's important to focus the message toward solutions and away from problems. Instead of merely admitting that a product is tainted, the company should move quickly to explain what it is doing, both to correct the immediate problem and to prevent its recurrence. It's not enough to say that questionable accounting occurred; instead, a company must say directly and specifically what it is doing to overcome the problems such practices created in both the short and longer terms.

Legal considerations play an obvious role in deciding what and how to communicate about a crisis. While the underlying issues are unsettled, it is generally agreed that a public admission of liability in, for example, a tainted product case can be used against the company in later proceedings. Working against this constraint is the need to take responsibility and lay out a plan of corrective action. Most companies who have experienced such crises find that the impact on sales from the damage to a corporate image resulting from perceived stonewalling exceeds the legal damages brought about by early and open admission of responsibility. A company's legal staff is rightly involved in shaping the messages around a crisis, but appearing to hide behind legal advice exacerbates controversy and creates opportunities for dangerous speculation. The company spokesperson who says, "On advice of counsel, I can't answer that question," is more likely to draw unnecessary attention to an issue than to calm excited listeners.

As with all communication, crisis communication calls for balance, common sense, and a strong awareness of audiences and intended outcomes. Legal constraints are real and need to be taken into account in responding to a crisis, but a clear message delivered quickly by a responsible official generally offers benefits far greater than those that result from an undue concern for potential liability. If the firm fails because public and employee confidence evaporates, legal damages become dramatically irrelevant.

Index

M

N

Q

R

S